Presence in the Modern World

PRESENCE
in the
MODERN WORLD

JACQUES ELLUL

A New Translation by Lisa Richmond

Foreword by Ted Lewis

Introduction to Jacques Ellul's Life and Thought by David W. Gill

CASCADE *Books* · Eugene, Oregon

PRESENCE IN THE MODERN WORLD
A New Translation

Copyright © 2016 Wipf and Stock Publishers. English translation copyright © 2016
Lisa Richmond. All rights reserved. Except for brief quotations in critical publica-
tions or reviews, no part of this book may be reproduced in any manner without
prior written permission from the publisher. Write: Permissions, Wipf and Stock
Publishers, 199 W. 8th Ave., Suite 3, Eugene, OR 97401.

Original french language edition of Jacques Ellul, *Présence au monde moderne*, copyright ©, and published by permission of, Editions de La Table Ronde. First edition
published by Éditions Roulet, 1948. Second edition published by Presses Bibliques
Universitaires, Éditions Ouverture, 1988.

Preface and afterword copyright Jacques Ellul, 1989. Used by permission of Helmers
& Howard Publishers, P.O. Box 7407, Colorado Springs, CO 80933.

Introduction to Jacques Ellul's Life and Thought copyright David W. Gill, 2016.

Cascade Books
An Imprint of Wipf and Stock Publishers
199 W. 8th Ave., Suite 3
Eugene, OR 97401

www.wipfandstock.com

PAPERBACK ISBN 13: 978-1-4982-9134-7
HARDCOVER ISBN 13: 978-1-4982-9136-1
EBOOK ISBN: 978-1-4982-9135-4

Cataloguing-in-Publication data:

Names: Ellul, Jacques.

Title: Presence in the modern world / Jacques Ellul, translated by Lisa Richmond, with a
    foreword by Ted Lewis and an introduction to Ellul's life and thought by David W. Gill.

Description: Eugene, OR: Cascade Books, 2016 | Includes bibliographical references and
    index.

Identifiers: ISBN 978-1-4982-9134-7 (paperback) | ISBN 978-1-4982-9136-1 (hardcover) |
    ISBN 978-1-4982-9135-4 (ebook)

Subjects: LCSH: Christian life. | Church and social problems. | Christian ethics. | Chris-
    tianity—20th century—Influence. | Church and the world. | Richmond, Lisa. | Lewis,
    Ted.| Gill, David W. | Title.

Classification: BV4501 E587 2016 (paperback) | BV4501 (ebook)

Manufactured in the U.S.A.   05/26/16

"In a real sense, [this] is Jacques Ellul's most astonishing book. . . . The book evidences an uncanny and virtually unerring perception of the forces and issues of contemporary social change which plague men and nations—and which, therefore, beset Christians in the world. Ellul not only anticipates the imminence of sophisticated technics, the dehumanizing tyrannies of mass media, and the perils of thermonuclear diplomacy, but also apprehends the relentless conflicts of ideologies among themselves and men, and then foresees a triumph of the totalitarian spirit, which has by now been substantially institutionalized in the United States and in Ellul's own country."

* * *

"In the theology of Ellul the recurrent and cosmic drama of the will to death is transcended, through the work of the Holy Spirit, by the will to life, bringing freedom from idolatry of death—in the form of nationalism, racism, ideology, personal lusts, class distinction, professionalism, or human philosophy. For Ellul, since death is real and the power of death is thus proved great, if not almighty, so is the Holy Spirit actualized in the everyday and immediate issues of existence by the emancipation from the power of death signaled in the resurrection—and dispensed so extravagantly thereby."

William Stringfellow
(from his Foreword to *The Presence of the Kingdom*, 1967).

Contents

Foreword

Readers of Jacques Ellul's magnum opus, *The Technological Society*, can hardly be faulted for concluding that his analysis of modern society is pessimistic and fatalistic. Nothing in society, so it seems, remains unsullied by the totalistic force of technique. But Ellul never intended this book to be understood in isolation from his other writings. In his 1981 essay "On Dialectic," he bemoaned the fact that, "No one is using my studies in correlation with one another." Perhaps it was a tall order for all of his readers, Christian and non-Christian alike, to appreciate the dialectical tension he established between his sociological works and his biblical or theological works. On the one hand, he was unveiling a dark vision of technological totalitarianism that pulls every facet of Western culture (and every person) into its vortex; on the other hand, he was presenting a theological vision where human freedom and responsibility could lead to a hopeful future. What all readers need to see, however, is how Ellul's social analysis was always *answered* by his biblical commentary, not in the sense that there are dogmatic religious answers, but rather in the sense of how divine revelation presents the opposite dialectical pole to technocracy. Indebted to Marx, Kierkegaard, and Barth for their respective dialectical methods, Ellul consistently worked within a framework where opposites do not synthesize but remain in a mid-zone of creative tension where awareness and social change can be stimulated.

It is in this dialectical framework that we can best appreciate the significance of Ellul's *Presence in the Modern World*. With the French edition coming out in 1948, this work can be seen as a blueprint for all of his later books. As Ellul later explained, the chapters grew out of four presentations he gave to a Christian audience in 1946. "I established the very broad plan for a work that would consist in studying the modern world and the Christian requirement in parallel," he said in 1989. "When I was writing this book, I had the impression that this was the direction that I needed to work in, and that this book could be the introduction to the whole." Likewise, Bernard Rordorf noted in his introduction to the second French edition that "this book announces Ellul's whole future body of work, bearing within itself the seed of that work's choices and developments." That seed, according to Rordorf, is Ellul's intentional duality, which "is the key for understanding Ellul's entire body of work." Even the original title (*Presence in the Modern World*) evokes the tension of this dialectic between spiritual and material realms.

Rejecting both Christian escapism from society and Christian collusion with society, Ellul set out to develop how Christians are to be *present* in a world with a style that is truly revolutionary. He repeatedly pointed out that Christian mission can be truly understood only in its confrontation with society. To do this, though, Ellul soon realized that he had to plumb the depths of modern society. "I needed to devote myself to discerning the foundations, structures, and components of the present 'age,' that is, the twentieth century" (Preface). And thus began the book that you now hold in your hands: Ellul's early sketchbook of social analysis, in conjunction with biblical reflection, which all together would find greater development in his subsequent writings. (Unless otherwise noted, all forthcoming quotes are by Ellul as translated in the chapters of this book.)

How might one who is not a Christian read a book that is wholly structured around the topic of *Christian presence* in the world? To begin with, Ellul's ideas largely grew out of his conversation with non-Christian sources. Without Marx, his extensive reconfiguration of the "End and Means" topic might not have unfolded. Without grappling with fascist or communist methods for manipulating facts, Ellul might not have developed his theories of propaganda that are foreshadowed in the chapter on "Communication." These two chapters, in fact, may serve as better starting points for readers who want to identify Ellul's early articulations of his social critique. While Ellul wrote specifically for the "Christian intellectual," he also wrote indirectly for all intellectuals who view themselves in "the time for awareness." Just as Christians must honestly see themselves "on the level of other human beings, along with them, subject to the same laws, influences, and despair," so those who are not Christians can also "wake up from this hideous nightmare in which techniques induce the world to slumber" and, according to Ellul, perhaps alter the course of social trends.

But is there anything, for Ellul, in *this* world that can help us to become aware and to become agents of real change? We are back to Ellul's pessimism. Humanity cannot generate its own illumination and remedy, especially in an age where novels such as *Brave New World* are written as prophetic literature about contemporary issues. Since the root problem of our mechanistic world is basically a spiritual one, the answer can only come in the "boundary between the profane and the sacred." Again, the Christian, as prophetic seer, is uniquely called to enter this border land between the dialectical poles of Babel and Christ, to "understand the decisive nature of our era." Awareness has to translate into action, of course, but never action that becomes the master. It is essentially "a matter of 'being' and not 'doing.'" For Ellul, this subversion of all other social agendas (which even Christians are prone to follow) is itself a revolutionary presence that strikes more to the core of technological totalitarianism than any other form of action.

Much of this boils down to the way ethics, for Ellul, is to be guided by a vision of God's future. The Christian mandate is not to save or change the world; it is to be, as Rordorf summarized it, "bearers of the eschaton, . . . bearers of the end that God desires." Being salt, light, and sheep in modern society is perhaps more revolutionary than anyone would suspect. Ellul drove home the point that authentic Christians live "on the margin of this totalitarian society, not by rejecting it outright but by sifting it thoroughly." It is very much in this context that we can see why such a prophet as William Stringfellow was invited to write the foreword for this book in 1967. Fittingly, he wrote that "*The Presence of the Kingdom* is Jacques Ellul's most astonishing book."

Given the exponential growth of technological trends, it may turn out that Christians will reach a place of radical witness only when they collaborate better with those who may not share a Christian faith but do share a commitment to reverse the slow drift of technological oppression. Such partners often have greater insights that can strengthen communities of Christian faith, and a book like this may lead to fruitful conversations for those who jointly want to move from enlightened comprehension to ethical response. Certainly Ellul's lifelong friendship with Bernard Charbonneau, who was not a Christian believer, represents this kind of dialectic partnership that stimulates new thought and subversive action. And if the subtitle of the original French edition is to be considered (*Présence au monde moderne: Problèmes de la civilisation post-chrétienne*), Christians and non-Christians alike face a crisis that requires all hands on deck. To be sure, this book shines the spotlight on the specific role that prophetic Christians have in this day and age. At the same time, Christians will likely falter in this role if they do not partner well with other co-prophets who equally wish to "give the slip" to modern civilization for the sake of true human freedom.

Ted Lewis
April 2016
Duluth, Minnesota

Translator's Preface

This foundational book by Jacques Ellul first appeared in French in 1948 under the title *Présence au monde moderne: Problèmes de la civilisation post-chrétienne* (Presence in the Modern World: Problems of Post-Christian Civilization). An English translation prepared by Olive Wyon was published in 1951 as *The Presence of the Kingdom* and was republished in 1967 and 1989. The French work was also republished, with minor revisions, in 1988. I have used this revised French version as the source for my translation.

My method in preparing this translation has been to incline toward the literal end of the translation spectrum while still seeking to produce a text that flows well in English. My goal has been to provide a clear expression of the original without crossing over into the kind of interpretation that should belong with the reader rather than the translator. At points where I found it necessary to explain or to supply words, I enclosed them in square brackets or provided a footnote.

An example of my method may be helpful. Here are two sentences from Ellul's original, accompanied by a very literal translation. Following this, I provide my translation as it appears in this book, and, for comparison, Olive Wyon's translation from 1951.

Mais	*en*	*fonction*	*de*	*cette*	*constatation,*	*quel*	*va*	*être*	*le*
But	in	function	of	this	observation,	what	is going	to be	the

rôle	*du*	*chrétien?* ...	*l'Écriture*	*même*	*nous*	*montre*
role	of the	Christian? ...	the Scripture	[it]self	to us	shows

comment	*rendre*	*cela*	*plus*	*réel,*	*comment*	*comprendre*
how	to render	that	more	real,	how	to understand

de	*façon*	*concrète*	*cette*	*situation*	*et*	*cette*	*action.*
in	fashion	concrete	this	situation	and	this	action.

[Richmond:] If all this is the case, what then is the Christian's role? ... Scripture itself shows us how to make the Christian's role more real and how to understand in a concrete way its situation and activity.

[Wyon:] If this, then, is the Christian's situation, what part should he play in the life of the world? ... It is the Bible which shows us what the Christian "calling" really is; it enables us to understand this situation, and it shows us what concrete action is required.

I frequently divided Ellul's long, syntactically loose sentences into more than one sentence. I changed paragraph breaks where I judged that such a change would promote greater understanding of the argument. I have chosen to leave apparent as much as possible various French expressions and ways of seeing the world. I think that English readers may find it interesting to learn, for example, that Huxley's *Brave New World* is known in French as *The Best of Worlds* (a reference to Voltaire's *Candide*), or that French has a verb *to tricolor*, which is roughly equivalent to *to wave the flag* (the French flag has three colors). Two requests of the publisher also governed my work: this translation uses gender-neutral language for human beings, and the French noun *technique* is rendered in English as *technique* rather than as *technics*.

Footnotes that comment on Ellul's main themes were provided by David Gill and are marked with the notation (DG). The remaining footnotes are my own. Ellul frequently referred to other writers or events. Most of the time, these references are not important for understanding his argument and can be disregarded.

I could not have prepared this translation without the help of others. I am grateful to Anne-Marie Andreasson-Hogg and to Eli Nupanga for reviewing portions of my text. To Don Simpson of Helmers & Howard, for permission to translate and print Ellul's preface and afterword to the 1989 English edition, and for copies of Ellul's typescripts of these. To Ted Lewis and David Gill, for their extensive collaboration and encouragement. Above all, I am grateful to Daniel Cérézuelle, whose knowledge and judgment are exceptional and who devoted his time to helping me improve this work. Of course, any errors that remain are my own.

Author's Preface

As a preface to this re-edition, about which I am very pleased, I would like to recall briefly the circumstances in which this book was written.

Before the war of 1939–45, European Christians were divided into two primary tendencies. For some, the only things that counted were witnessing, evangelism, theology, Bible study, and piety. And most of these, including the Barthians,[1] believed that if God does everything, then we need not be concerned with the world's history. The other group believed on the contrary that it was essential to intervene in the concrete, practical, and essentially political world. (A very small number in France, around André Philip, pursued a Christian socialism.[2]) For this group, the one great problem raised was that of the state in general (and in this, they were good followers of Karl Barth!). What were the powers, functions, and limits of the state? It is true that at this time people were coming up against the establishment of great dictatorships, and the question that seemed urgent and perhaps unprecedented was to know precisely what position to take in the face of this dictatorial state. Was it always necessary, for instance, to obey Romans 13:1 and following (which, regardless of the political issue, always seemed to be "the text" that was absolutely clear and provided the sole orientation for Christian conduct)?

But in my own case, the conditions of my early life, my encounter with the thought of Karl Marx, and then my studies in law, economics, and history, all drove me to refuse both of these positions.[3] The first, because it seemed to me to fit the criticisms of unbelievers: religion serves only

1. Followers of the theology of Karl Barth (1886–1968).

2. André Philip (1920–70), Protestant socialist politician.

3. Karl Marx (1818–83), theorist of revolutionary socialism.

as an escape from the world. As for the second, I certainly did not have enough biblical knowledge to critique it, but it seemed to me impossible to defend. I was already forming the very sharp distinction between the powers, the authorities (still very personalized, very incarnated in a person) and the modern, completely abstract state. In addition, the state was *one* of the elements that made up this complex world, and I saw with a certain impatience that Christians either left things to happen on their own or else were mistaken about the problem. I had been part of two movements, one Catholic (*Esprit*) and the other Protestant (*Ordre Nouveau*), in which others shared my same concerns, but none of this carried over into [broader] Christian settings.[4] It was during this time that some friends and I studied the new facts of the large city, mechanization, and then technique, administration[5] (which would later become bureaucracy!), and so on . . .

* * *

When the war came, Protestants' choices and matters for thought seemed very clear and simple, at least in France. (The situation was more difficult for Catholics, because Marshal Pétain was a great Catholic who privileged the Catholic Church, and the "values" that he proposed for France's motto, "Work, Family, Homeland," corresponded well to Catholic values.[6]) For us, it was *clear* that Hiterlism had to be opposed, that it was no longer enough to hold [only] a theologian's or devout layperson's position toward it, and that we needed to engage in the fight (and as a result, "do politics"). So this was the terrible adventure that led so many French Protestants to take politics seriously. I was always convinced that this was not enough, but there was an "order of urgency"—we first had to overcome Nazism and fascism. After that . . . we would see!

But at the Liberation,[7] I found my friends divided again into two groups. On the one side were those for whom the important thing was to return to theology and building up the church. On the other were those who had a passion for politics and no longer thought about anything else

---

4. *Esprit* (Spirit) and *Ordre nouveau* (New Order) were associations and periodicals of the personalist movement. See note 8, p. 95.

5. That is, the overall work of government through its departments and services.

6. Philippe Pétain (1856–1951), head of the French Vichy government under the Nazi occupation of 1940–44.

7. The end of the Nazi occupation of France in 1944.

(even in their pastoral ministry). But it was a very specific sort of politics that concerned them. In the Resistance,[8] they had met and become friends with many communists, and from that point on they viewed politics only from this perspective. I believe that their fixation on communism happened all the more easily in fact because, before the war, they had not had any political experience or even any political ideas.

So then in 1945, I realized that I had to write a short and simple little book about the presence of the Christian in the world of today. Not in the world in general, but in the world as it was, by trying to broaden the political view, enable the complexity of problems to be felt, and take new social phenomena into account. Christians and the church could not hold themselves aloof from the history of human beings, but neither could they become assimilated into one of the political currents (which too often had been the case throughout the church's history). Nor could they succumb to the temptation of wanting to elaborate a Christian society, a Christian state, a Christian politics. These were the three impossibilities that I found myself facing and that required a new investigation.

* * *

I carried out this investigation with groups of non-conformist students[9] that I brought together and with whom I went on camping trips. But the thinking was still only fragmentary, usually based on what met their concerns. When the Ecumenical Institute at Bossey[10] asked me in 1946 to give four talks on "the Christian in modern society," I was given the opportunity to attempt a synthesis. I had to take a side implicitly in the theological opposition between Barth and Emil Brunner[11] (who had a great influence at that time), and also in relation to Barth's position in favor of a political expression of socialism.[12] (At this time Barth had entirely lost his sharpness of judgment, mostly due to the influence of his friend Fritz Lieb, a great admirer of the USSR and supporter of communism.)

8. The collective name for efforts to defeat or undermine the Nazi occupation. Ellul participated in the Resistance.

9. Student groups in the 1930s, affiliated with the personalist movement.

10. A study center near Geneva, run by the World Council of Churches.

11. Emil Brunner (1889–1966), theologian.

12. Ellul's typescript reads: *en faveur du socialisme comme expression politique du socialisme* (in favor of socialism as a political expression of socialism).

My four talks resulted in lively discussions. I felt even more strongly that I ought to press ahead with my analysis of society along with a rigorous biblical understanding that would not make concessions to various possible methods of interpretation. I began writing up these four talks and divided them into two parts. I have said elsewhere that many years previously I established the very broad plan for a work that would consist in studying the modern world and the Christian requirement in parallel. When I was writing this book, I had the impression that this was the direction that I needed to work in, and that this book could be the introduction to the whole. An incident confirmed this: my friends' pastor, J. Gastambide,[13] said to me one day, "This is very interesting, but you often limit yourself to asserting things; you don't demonstrate them. For example, what you say about technique is new, but you need to develop it to give proof." It was after this remark that I began to work on my book about technique, and "that's how it all began."

* * *

But I still needed a key to serve as a guide or compass and also as an intellectual instrument! As I hesitated among several themes and approaches, I was struck by the verse of Paul: "Do not be conformed to the present age, but be transformed by the renewing of the mind, so that you may discern the will of God, what is good, gives him pleasure, and is well done" (Rom 12:2). There were in this text three imperatives for me that I had to try to follow from that point on, and that I had to find ways of approaching that fit the situation today.

"Do not be conformed to the present age." There are two possible conformities. The first is voluntary adherence (and for this, it was enough to understand political programs, economic plans, and doctrines). But what drew me more, and what seemed to me to fit the level of Paul's thinking, was unconscious, involuntary adherence—which is so evident in this present age that we don't even think about it: these unspoken rules, taboos, and unquestioned truths that form a group's unconscious and subconscious. The "present age" is filled with evidence of this. But I completely rejected

---

13. Jean Gastambide (1906–88), a pastor in the Reformed Church of France and a signer of the Pomeyrol Theses, a Christian statement against Nazi collaborationism and antisemitism similar to the Barmen Declaration.

the interpretation by which this "present age" (*aiōn*[14]) is a kind of meta-physical reality, opposed to the coming kingdom, and always the same in itself. This present age was neither the particular one that Paul inhabited, nor a mysterious entity that was always the same; to me, each generation needed to recognize that it concerns its *own* age. So I needed to devote myself to discerning the foundations, structures, and components of the present "age," . . . that is, the twentieth century. To do this, it would be necessary to understand the most important facts and also to interpret them accurately. But the "scientific" method of the "social sciences" (including mathematical treatment) seemed inadequate to me. I preferred a method closer to that of Marx, and especially, Weber.[15] This is how I chose the questions that I addressed in this book.

Then, once we understand what this age is made of, we must, as Paul says, "not be conformed," that is, not "take on the form" of this age. This is how I understood it: We must not follow everyone's opinion, not *adapt* ourselves to the powers of this age, not follow the "conformisms," be they political, philosophical, or ideological, nor the trends—even when these ideologies and trends *seemed* to conform to the gospel (for example, favoring the poor, decolonization, etc.). In general, such "similarities" arose from a lack of understanding about our society or a highly superficial interpretation of the biblical message. Some Christians believed they were Good Samaritans by helping the poor (but they did not see the specific details of poverty today), or they believed they were being like Jesus by becoming involved in violent movements, but they were and are still wrong about revolution. So I had to begin by understanding the structures of our society that determined the conformisms. I had to critique them, starting from the gospel, and become engaged in a movement in which I would necessarily be alone, because it would be based in faith in a revelation that others did not share. In order to change the world, beginning with changing our "form," we were alone. But if all Christians understood this, the world would actually be transformed through the action of the Holy Spirit.

What I have just described ("Do not be conformed") could not be based in a particular understanding or specialized knowledge. It was the "renewing of your mind," meaning that the starting point lies above the

14. A Greek word meaning *era* or *age*. Paul uses this word throughout his New Testament writings in reference to the world's path apart from Christ. In 2 Cor 4:4, Paul says that Satan is the ruler of the *aiōn*.

15. Max Weber (1864–1920), sociologist.

action that I just described. It requires a change in our understanding about things, people, and situations (which is more than a change in method!), meaning that everything must be brought into the light of Jesus Christ. This involves a *clarity* that the best observers never attain, and which was actually that of the prophets, and *a new way of understanding*. For me, this renewing of the mind corresponded, then, to the commandment to love God with . . . all one's mind. It seemed to me that it did not mean: Do theology and become a pastor! To love God with one's mind meant putting one's thinking in the service of God's action in the world, through the medium of the believer.

And this service related as much to politics as to psychological action! What good news[16] today for transforming minds as well as hearts, through which the world could be changed. And this change of the mind should ultimately correspond to what God desires for this world, be pleasing to God, and be *well done*. So, for example, a revolution for justice that caused millions of deaths could not be pleasing to God or "be well done." Multiplying communication in order to have nothing to say could not correspond to loving one's neighbor. (The theory of relations did not yet exist that would enable people to "love" not only those close to them but also those far away, which is a complete misunderstanding of *agapē*.[17]) New light would always need to be shed, corresponding to an understanding of the Bible in the "here and now." I asked myself, if we must take this decisive verse seriously, what then might be the Christian's position, or "side," in the world?

Such were the issues for which I posed the question of the Christian's presence in this world, a new world in comparison to what had existed before the war. This was the starting point for all that followed.

---

16. *Évangile*, gospel.

17. A Greek word meaning *love*, found extensively throughout the New Testament. It refers to love of the kind that God has for human beings and that they, through him, may have for him and for one another. See for example Matt 22:36–39, Rom 5:8, and 1 Cor 13.

CHAPTER ONE

The Christian in the World

1

As we begin these studies, it seems needful to start from a few biblical truths that are well known by everyone, yet never entirely useless to recall.

Scripture tells us that Christians are in the world and that there they should remain. Christians are not meant to be separate or to set themselves apart. Such separation is for God to effect at the end of time, when he will gather the wheat and discard the chaff[1]; it is never for human beings to decide their own election. Similarly, Christians ought not to live as a group, associating among themselves and ultimately refusing to associate with others. Christian gatherings should never be exclusive. Yet if Christians are thus necessarily in the world, they are not of it. This means that their mind, life, and heart are not ruled by the world and do not depend on it. They belong to another master. As Christians belong in this way to him, this master sends them out into the world while still keeping them in communion with him.[2]

But this communion with Jesus Christ entails very serious consequences. First, it brings Christians face to face with the world's spiritual

---

1. Matt 3:12; Luke 3:17.
2. John 17:11–18.

reality, not its material might. Because they are in communion with Jesus Christ, they struggle not against flesh and blood but against "thrones, powers, dominations." This communion also assures them that they do not belong to the world. They are free from the fate of the world, which is heading toward death. With this freedom that comes through grace, they *are able* to struggle against the world's spiritual realities. To be precise, they are called to destroy the fate that oppresses the world, and they are able to destroy it. God's grace provides them with the arms they need (Eph 6:10–20).

If all this is the case, what then is the Christian's role? It is too easy to reply: to witness, evangelize, lead a Christian life, or act according to God's will. All that is true, but as long as it is not seriously understood and remains merely a traditional formulation, it does not lead us to the truth of anything. In fact, Scripture itself shows us how to make the Christian's role more real and how to understand in a concrete way its situation and activity.

Christians must not act like just anyone. They have a role in the world that no one else can fill. They are not called on to select the human activities that they consider good and then participate in them. They are not called on to bless any natural enterprise or support any human decision. They are charged with a mission that is unknown to people in their natural condition.[3] This mission is what is ultimately decisive for all human action. From this mission all the truth or error of their actions derives.

If Christians work with all their might for a human project, they are only human beings like others and their effort has no added value. But if they accept their specific function as Christians, which does not necessarily involve participating in the world in material or measurable ways, then this is decisive for human history.

God has not sent them for any other reason than to carry out this function that is entirely different from the others. The world cannot understand it, yet the meaning of all other functions depends on this one. Scripture describes it in three ways:

> *You are the salt of the earth.*
> *You are the light of the world.*
> *I send you out as sheep among wolves.*[4]

To be the salt of the earth refers specifically to Leviticus 2:13, where we are told that salt is the sign of the covenant. This means that Christians

---

3. *L'homme naturel*, the natural man. See 1 Cor 2:14.
4. Matt 5:13–14; 10:16; Luke 10:3.

stand before humankind, within the world's spiritual reality, as the visible sign of the new covenant that God has made with this world in Jesus Christ. Christians must be a true sign, however: their life and words must manifest this covenant to humankind. Otherwise the earth feels itself bereft of covenant. It no longer knows where it is headed and lacks any possible self-understanding or certainty as to its preservation. This fact of being the salt of the earth is the primary way by which Christians are involved in the world's preservation, much more than by any material activity.

To be the light of the world: the light appeared in the darkness, but the darkness did not overcome it.[5] Christians are this light in Christ. The statement has a twofold meaning. First, light is what dispels darkness, separates life from death, and provides the criterion of goodness (this is why in the biblical text a reference to good works directly follows this sentence). Apart from this light, we cannot strictly know what is a good work or the good in itself.

In another sense, this light of the world is what gives meaning to the world's history, what orients and explains it. As a mere sequence of events, the course of history reveals no logic or certainty. The logic emerges through the church's presence, as odd as this may seem. This is why Christians, by being light, are a factor in the world's life. In addition to their work of preserving the world, Christians are instruments of revelation and bear witness to salvation.

As sheep among wolves: here again Christians are the sign of the reality of God's action. The lamb of God is Jesus Christ, who takes away the sins of the world.[6] But all Christians are treated as their master is, and all Christians receive from Jesus Christ a share in his work. They are sheep not because their action or sacrifice has a purifying effect on the world, but because in the world's midst they are the true, living, and ever renewed sign of the sacrifice of the lamb of God. In the world, everyone seeks to be a wolf; no one is assigned to play the sheep's role. Yet the world cannot survive if no one bears living witness to this sacrifice. This is why it is essential for Christians to guard against being wolves *spiritually*, that is, spiritual dominators. Christians must accept others' domination over them and daily sacrifice their lives, reflecting in this way the sacrifice of Jesus Christ.

These biblical expressions should not be understood as similes or special terms to use when speaking of Christians. They are not figures of

5. John 1:5.
6. John 1:29.

speech or pretty pictures. We are much too inclined to see only fine phrases and poetry. Nor are they a sort of accident that can happen to Christians, a possibility; we speak too easily as though Christians happen to have this quality but could have others.

Instead, these biblical expressions convey a stark and unavoidable reality. Jesus Christ brings us face to face with the Christian's particular function—and we can have no other. Christians cannot be otherwise, they do not have the choice. If they are not like this, they are not fulfilling their role and are betraying Jesus Christ and the world also. Christians can always strive to do good works and exhaust themselves in religious or social activity, but this will signify absolutely nothing if they do not accomplish the one mission that Jesus Christ charges them with specifically—to be, first, a sign.

* * *

This is the situation of all Christians. It is most acute for the laity, however, because for them in particular there is no separation from the world. They can have no illusions on this score. In the first place, they participate in the world through their work and concerns. The world constantly assails their very being. Claiming to be separate becomes more and more difficult, as each person is forced into a world that becomes more intrusive, crushing, and demanding than ever. Our occupations alone are enough today to absorb all of our resources. Each of us is drowning in overwhelming activity, leaving us no time to reflect, carry out our function as a Christian, or even live.

And just as laypeople are not free to lead their lives as they wish, they are also subject to a mechanical solidarity that entirely prevents them from making even a pretense of faith.[7] Whether they wish to or not, they are obliged to live like others—much more so, materially speaking, today than

7. The French noun *solidarité* may refer to joining with others in movements for political or social change (the typical meaning of *solidarity* in English), but it also refers more generally to social ties, mutual responsibility, and interdependence. Given its wide range of meaning, the word is expressed variously throughout this translation. As concerns *mechanical solidarity*, in his *De la division du travail social* (On the Division of Work in Society), the sociologist Emile Durkheim (1858–1917) described *solidarité mécanique* as the social cohesion or conformity that arises from a shared way of life, and he described *solidarité organique* as that which arises in modern societies from functional complementarity and specialization.

in previous civilizations. Isolation or separation is no longer possible. The illusion has vanished that the Christian life [can be lived] within a convent or hermitage. Whether due to the simple material fact of modern transportation systems, the interconnection of economic institutions, or the rise of democracy—in any case, influences are at work to constrain people in this conformity.

Thus Christians cannot consider themselves pure in comparison with others or declare themselves unaffected by the world's sin. A major fact of our civilization is that sin is becoming more and more collective, and each individual person is constrained to participate in it. Each one bears the consequences of others' transgressions. This is particularly true in war, for example, but it is the same in all other social situations. The illusion is passing away that one can be "perfect" in the midst of a lost world.

People today can no longer have confidence in the virtues of individuals, in their goodness or energy, precisely because they no longer face individual sins but the state of human sin as a whole. This ancient biblical truth is now striking to all. Our society irrefutably manifests God's revelation of our sin. There is no one righteous, no, not one (Rom 3:10). This is not because each person as an individual is wicked, but because all things are confined under sin (Gal 3:22). This mutual relation in sin extends across space and time, linking us with those who have died in their sin, back to original sin itself. What our contemporary world teaches us is that this doctrine is not an idea or an academic discussion but the recognition of a reality that is as concrete as each person's complicity in modern warfare.

This situation is unpleasant for Christians. Priests or pastors feel it less directly, but the laity cannot escape from it. They do all they can to escape, however, and we find two ways in which this is attempted. Some try to separate the spiritual situation from the material. By divesting the material situation of significance, they declare it to be neutral and irrelevant to eternal life. They then fix their attention on "spiritual problems" alone. What counts, they say, is the inner life: to be salt or light is a purely spiritual affirmation with no practical consequences.

This attitude is just what Jesus Christ calls hypocrisy. It means that we give up living out our faith within the world. It means that we turn the living person of Jesus Christ into an abstraction. God became incarnate; it is not our job to disincarnate him. This division of our lives into two domains—one spiritual, in which we are perfect, and the other material (without importance!), in which we are "like everyone else"—is one of the reasons why the churches' influence in the world is waning. This flight from the responsibility of faith is of course a convenient solution for the intolerable situation that our society places us in. But it is just the opposite of what Jesus Christ wants for us and what he came to accomplish.

Another solution, more common today, consists in wanting to moralize or Christianize the world's activity. If the state were Christian, how agreeable it would be to rely on it. Let us therefore create a Christian state—and so on. . . . It is a case here of having a sort of "Christian notion" of things, having good institutions and moral standards, identifying the good in each thing, and applying this coating over our world's situation. Daub the devil in gilt, dress him up in white; perhaps he will become an angel. Such is the whitewash that all Christian moralities, sociologies, and politics, even Social Christianity, offer us as the solution.[8] They try to tinge the world's activities and conditions with a Christian hue, either by using a convenient theology to explain and justify them, or by pronouncing a blessing over them, or by seeking to apply Christian remedies and virtues.

In short, in each case we try to make acceptable the situation that the world puts us in. In the same way that we try to demonstrate that we can be a soldier or a banker *and* a Christian, we perform good works in order to acquit ourselves of social disorder and human misery. By all these means, we try to reach the point where the world's condition does not offend Christian "conscience" *too* deeply. In reality, what we want is to construct a bridge between the world and the kingdom of God, where Christians could then locate themselves permanently. Clearly, this bridge is morality, along with good works and a good conscience.

But this attempt to end the scandal that the world must be for faith, and that faith must be for the world, turns out to be the most anti-Christian position possible. In the study that follows, we will examine exactly how Christians are implicated, what their situation is, in the face of some of the profound problems that the world presents. But we will also see how in fact there is no possible solution, understood in terms of relief or satisfaction.

8. *Christianisme social*, a French religious movement that arose in the nineteenth century, seeking to improve social conditions. A similar movement in the United States is the social gospel of Washington Gladden (1836–1918) and Walter Rauschenbusch (1861–1918). Ellul resists any tendency to reduce the Christian faith to a this-worldly formula for social reform. (DG)

2

From what angle then should the question be considered? Our task here is not to say anything at all novel but simply to rediscover what has always been a perfectly well-known Christian truth—one that Christians always strive to forget, because it is very embarrassing, even intolerable. The first element of this situation is precisely that it is not a matter of attenuating the opposition between Christian faith, what revelation requires, and life in the world with its own demands, faults, and compromises.

The fact of living in the world, which we must not evade, is a scandal for our faith. It must be and remain a scandal. We have no right to accustom ourselves to this world or spread a veil of Christian illusion over it. By living in the world, we live in the domain of Satan, the prince of this world.[9] What we see all around us is this prince's constant activity and the consequences of the sinful condition affecting each one of us. For despite all our efforts and piety, we participate in the world's sin. We participate because, despite our faith, we are and remain sinners (*semper peccator et justus*[10]) and also because we are linked with others in the communities that God has instituted. When a member of my family or nation commits a sin, I am responsible before God for this transgression. This truth must not remain just a verbal one.

We need to understand what this participation in the world actually means. To do so we must consider not only our individual sin but also our sin that comes from living in the world and being implicated in it. We must stop believing therefore that our virtues can offset our sins. We must stop believing that an accommodation with the world is possible, such that humankind could be less wicked, if not less unhappy, living in it. At the same time, if we take seriously our situation as Christians, we must refuse to reconcile ourselves to the world's corruption. We must not tell ourselves that we can do nothing about it. To speak in this way . . . is to play into the hands of the prince of this world!

9. Through his writings, Ellul freely refers to this mysterious but powerful enemy of freedom and humanity. He distinguishes Satan, the Accuser, from the devil, the Divider. "The Satan is only the composite, the synthesis, the sum total of all the accusations brought by people against other people in the world. There is no 'spirit' independent of a person that would 'inspire' him to bring this accusation. It wells up from man's heart all by itself." Ellul, *If You Are the Son of God*, 8–9. (DG)

10. Latin for *always sinner and justified*. A reference to Martin Luther's commentary on Rom 12:2. For the English, see *Luther's Works*, 25:434 (Saint Louis, 1972). For the original Latin, see *D. Martin Luthers Werke*, 56:442 (Weimar, 1938, reprinted 2007).

Thus we are caught between two necessities that form an unresolvable tension. On the one hand, we cannot make this world less sinful; on the other, we cannot accept it as it is. To reject either side is to reject the actual situation in which God has placed those whom he sends into the world. Just as we are caught in the tension between sin and grace, so also are we caught between these two contradictory demands. It is an infinitely painful position, it is very uncomfortable, but it is the only one that can be fruitful and faithful for the Christian's action and presence in the world.

This tension must first be accepted and then lived out continuously. We must accept, in repentance, what is irreducibly scandalous about our life in the world, recognizing that it cannot be otherwise. To claim that it can be otherwise is hypocrisy! But to truly recognize our situation in the world assumes that we truly understand its problems. To be honest, we cannot accept this tension of the Christian life as an abstract truth. We have to live it, and bring it to life in the most concrete and vital way possible. And besides, Christians must understand that bringing this tension to life is the only real way to help the world on the social, economic, and political level.

In fields such as these, the world typically presents false problems. People in their natural condition are incapable on their own of seeing the spiritual reality within which they struggle. They see only what appear to be social, political, or economic problems, and they try to work within this appearance using technical means and moral criteria. In this way they end up in situations that are always more false and complicated, until what they have called their civilization reaches the point of collapse.

In such situations, the Christian's role will be precisely not to formulate the problems as others do, not to attempt futile technical and moral solutions, but to succeed in discovering the actual spiritual difficulties that any political or economic situation involves. As for the solution, it cannot be in any way based on calculation. It can be only a way of life and the acceptance of a forgiveness, for these sins too, granted in Christ Jesus. In other words, it is by living and receiving the gospel that political, economic, and other problems can be resolved. Only by accepting the tension described above can we respond to them in a human way that is not a lie or pretense.

Besides, the fact that the laity will accept this tension in their lives, and live it out to the full, is the necessary human condition for theology to find a voice by which to address the world. It is the true price to pay so that there can be contact between the language of faith and that of pagans. In reality, theologians today no longer have anything to say to the world because the laity no longer exist in our churches. On the one side there is the pastor who does not understand the world's situation, and on the other there are laypeople who go about carefully keeping their faith separate from their life or trying to get by with a moral system. Theological truth has no point of encounter with the world.

To say this is not to doubt that the Holy Spirit, he alone, assuredly establishes the connection, but it is to recognize that in the entire course of God's action in history he uses a material medium, a human means, to act by his Spirit. This material medium is exactly what is lacking in our churches, and this is why the Word that has been proclaimed, the gospel, no longer affects the world. This medium is the laity living out the tension described above. They are the point of encounter between the world's ideologies, in the midst of which they live, and theology—between economic realities and Jesus Christ's forgiveness for these realities that absolutely cannot be "improved" in some other way before God. It could almost be said that the lay Christian's experience is the ground for the theologian's human understanding.

Laypeople are not "guinea pigs," however. When they live out this tension each day of their lives, their very presence leads the church to recognize the value and truth of the world's distress and leads the world to recognize its true problems beneath the lies that it strives to perpetuate so that it does not hear the Word of God. Thus the position of the layperson's life is essential for the church and for the world. It would be best therefore not to distort it.

* * *

But this does not exhaust the real problem of Christians' situation in the world. They must try to live out what it means in daily life to be "salt of the earth," "light of the world," "sheep among wolves." This must not remain a set of formulas but take on a living and concrete shape. It must become a fact of life.

This is in fact the problem of Christian ethics that is being raised, ethics that has nothing to do with morality, generally so called, and even less to do with "Christian" virtues as traditionally understood.[11] It is clear that

---

11. The Christian virtues, or positive traits of character, have typically been understood as dispositions, inclinations, capabilities, and habits that are given, even "infused," by God. Besides Jesus' beatitudes in Matt 5 and the fruit of the Spirit in Gal 5, Paul's

Christian ethics cannot be known by applying theological judgments or intellectual constructs, even when they are based in revelation and faith. At the center of Christian ethics is a battle of individual faith before God, a living attitude that is held according to each person's measure of faith and as a result of faith. It is never a set of rules, formulas, or watchwords, and all Christians are in fact responsible for their works and conscience. So we can never draw up a description of God's ethical demand that is complete and valid for everyone, any more than we can reach its center. We can only trace its outline and conditions and study its basic elements by way of examples.[12]

At the center, in fact, lies this idea that Christian ethics rests on an agonistic structure of life, meaning that the Christian life is a continual struggle, a decisive and ultimate fight. This is nothing else than the constant and actual presence in our hearts of both judgment and grace. Yet this fact is precisely what assures our freedom. We are free because at each moment of our lives we are under both judgment and grace—and thus we are placed in a new situation, one that has no predetermined program or satanic fetters. To go further belongs to the theologian, but this much is enough to show us that the whole Christian attitude has a direct relation to God's action in Jesus Christ.

The two primary characteristics of this ethics, it seems to me, are that it must be temporary, and that it is apologetic. *Temporary*, because it concerns specific, variable situations. Ethics is not a matter of formulating principles but of knowing how to evaluate an action in particular circumstances. This means that we do not have to confine ourselves to unvarying moral concepts. Scripture teaches us that ethics does vary in its form and practical applications according to place and situation. This may be surprising after

---

"faith, hope, and love" in 1 Cor 13 are understood as the core Christian virtues. Ellul objects to viewing them as acquired, stable conditions. His view is more existential: hope and faith are more accurately *stances* that we take on, before God and in this moment. In response, God gives us freedom and holiness. (DG)

12. Ellul's introduction to ethics is *To Will and To Do*, in which he develops a stark contrast between the "moralities" (theoretical and actual) of the world and the existentialist Christian ethics of the Word. He explores hope in *Hope in Time of Abandonment* and in *The Ethics of Freedom*, which corresponds to hope. Ellul then explores faith in *Living Faith*. He drafted a thousand pages on the ethics of holiness as a response to faith, which has not yet been edited or published. Faith binds us to Christ, and this separates us from the world and makes us holy and distinctive. Ellul wrote several essays on love, the third virtue, but not a full-length study. He did not write his ethics of relationship, which corresponds to love in his schema. This was the ethics project that he announced and that he believed to be essential for both the church and the world. (DG)

what I said above about the center of ethics. One might conclude that no givens or structures exist, that ethics consists simply in letting Christians act according to their faith. In fact this is not the case. Faith has implications that can be objectively elaborated. To say the contrary is to engage in angelism—to believe that we are already in the kingdom of God and that our flesh no longer offers any resistance to the action of the Spirit. Instead, we are still in this "body of death."[13]

Constructing a Christian ethic is necessary, first, because it is a guide, a pointer given to faith, a true help to brothers and sisters. It also enables us to provide real, practical content to the judgment that God passes on us. And finally, it is needed for the edification of the church. But such elaboration must not substitute for the combat of faith within each Christian. This is why it is a guide and not a requirement. We should not view this ethics as providing the permanent solution to all problems. It must be in essence temporary and continually subject to question, review, and reformulation through the efforts of the whole church community.

Ethics is, next, necessarily *apologetic*. But this should not be understood in the usual sense of defending and explaining Christian truth, that is, as an intellectual exercise. Apologetics, which actually cannot be carried out by human beings, is described in Matthew 5:16: "Let your light shine before men so that they may see your good works and glorify your Father." In other words, works done by virtue of or as a result of ethics should appear in the light of Jesus Christ as true good works. The world is incapable of recognizing these good works on its own; it can do so only when enlightened in this way. Our works should flow so directly from the action of Jesus Christ in us that Christ's action illuminates our works for the world.

This implies that we ought not to take the world's judgment as our reference point in determining what we should do. Instead, our works are what should elicit such judgment. And these works should lead people to give praise to God. In this way they have an apologetic character. Our whole ethics is meaningless if it is not oriented toward this combat with the world that should result in the glory of God. Ethics as the church constructs it should thus be a precise expression of the tension that is each Christian's situation. It is the picture of this combat, and the purpose of ethics is to direct this combat toward God's glorification. Thus we see that ethics is inseparable from the preaching of the Word, because Christians' actual

---

13. Rom 7:24.

behavior truly destroys the work of Satan and contributes to the edification of the body of Christ in the world.

But in closing, we must return to this idea that ethics is not a means of resolving Christian tension. It is not a formula for how to live uprightly. It is not a synthesis of Christian faith and the world's values. It is not an ability given to Christians for living without the Holy Spirit. It is exactly the opposite of all these.

This problem of ethics does not encompass Christians' entire situation in the world. In short, it is concerned only with describing their action. This action is however only one factor that comes between the "situation"[14] (the tension to be accepted, as we have seen above) and involvement in the world's preservation, which is a fruit of the application of ethics.

* * *

Christians must participate in the world's preservation. They really must work toward it. But again we must try to dispel serious misunderstanding on this subject. When we speak of the world's preservation, we immediately envision involvement in the activities that the world considers best for itself. The world chooses its paths and determines its plan of action for resolving its problems. It is often thought that Christians, to help preserve the world, should make efforts along these lines.

Thus when we were appalled by Hitler's diabolical program, the crusade was preached.[15] The world took up arms, and Christians took up these same arms and fought against this demonic power just as others did. In the same way today, when the problem of reconstruction[16] has arisen, many Christians, even the best ones, advocate this same reconstruction and urge people along the path that the world has chosen. They say that the United Nations is an admirable institution and the way of the future, that what matters most is producing material goods, and that prefabricated housing is the solution for everything. I have even seen in a very Christian (Catholic) magazine that "the washing machine could be a means of France's salvation!"

The confusion here seems to me serious and weighty. Christians participate truly in the world's preservation not by acting like others and

---

14. La *"mise en situation,"* the state of being in a situation, setting, or context.

15. That is, people spoke out forcefully about resisting Hitler.

16. The effort of recovery and rebuilding after World War II.

laboring at the world's technical tasks but by fulfilling their specific role as described above. This does not mean that technical work should not be done, or that it is useless. No, the point is that everyone does this kind of work, and it has no meaning if it is not guided, accompanied, and sustained by another work, one that Christians alone can do and yet often do not. For the world must be preserved by the ways of God and not by the technique of human beings (although technique can enter into the ways of God if we take care to hold it under judgment and submission).[17] And the world must be preserved according to a certain order willed by God and not by the plan that human beings create from this order (although such a plan can be acceptable to God if we concern ourselves with a certain truth, an authentic justice).

This is why, in facing up to Hitler, if it is true that he represented a satanic power, there was *first* a spiritual battle to wage. Prayer is what should have been decisive, but we no longer have confidence in the extraordinary power of prayer! Prayer was the exorcism that drives out demons by the Holy Spirit, the armor of faith. It is quite possible that if Christians had truly acted according to these means, while everyone else was thinking of material warfare (which was *also* necessary) or simply of blessing the guns, the result would not have been this horrifying triumph of the Hitlerian spirit that we see now throughout the world.

The world today is reaping what Christians have sown. In the face of spiritual peril, Christians called "to arms!" and fought materially. Materially triumphant, we are spiritually vanquished. Only Christians could have waged spiritual battle, but they did not do so. They did not fulfill their role in the preservation of the world.

And today we are witnessing the same error with reconstruction. Christians and churches have first to do a spiritual kind of work, a work of realizing the world's true situation, seeking after and preaching the order of God, Christian reconstruction, and the formation of a civilization that is on the right level for human beings. This is a work precisely within the real possibility of the church. Everything else is futile if that is not accomplished. Everything else can lead only to more disorder.

It seems to me that this participation, which is both real and specific for the world's preservation, can lead to the idea of redeeming the time. If

---

17. Ellul's most famous book is *The Technological Society*. Technique, the root of technology, refers to rational, scientific, measurable methods of doing something in the most efficient way possible. See chapter three, below, on ends and means. (DG)

we put the two texts of Colossians 4:5 and Ephesians 5:15 side by side, we see that they are constructed in the very same fashion and the progression of Paul's thought is clear:

Colossians 4:5–6	Ephesians 5:15–17
Walk in wisdom toward those who are outside.	See that you walk circumspectly, as the wise.
Redeem the time.	Redeem the time.
Let your speech always be accompanied by grace, seasoned with salt.	Understand what the will of the Lord is.

Even without trying to enter further into the problem of redeeming the time, the idea of time as enslaved and needing redemption to be set free, we need only observe that what we have here is a remarkably vital indication for studying the Christian's situation in the world. This indication seems to lie at the very center of this problem, because it is placed, one could say, at the pivot point between conduct (thus the question of ethics) and preaching—between good works, which are the fruit of wisdom, and the knowledge of God's will. So we cannot avoid considering this idea of redeeming the time, for the very reason that it is presented *on the level of the Christian's situation* (and not in its theological aspect), at the center of the Christian life, as being the particular and decisive Christian function that encompasses all that we have said to this point. In any case, these texts show us that there can be no separation between preaching and behavior. To redeem the time is both a work of preservation (and this is indeed the work of authentic preservation) and a work of salvation, because no more separation exists here. This situation of Christians in the world appears then as singularly charged with meaning, if we consider that it is on their behavior and preaching (or simply on their witness) that the redemption of time depends.

* * *

One aspect remains to be considered as we broach the concrete nature of this situation. To participate truly in this preservation of the world, Christians must place themselves at the meeting point between two currents: the Lord's will, and that of the world.

The will of the Lord, appearing as both judgment and forgiveness, law and grace, commandment and promise, is revealed to us in Scripture, illuminated by the Spirit of God. It has to be explicated in the present time, but it does not vary. This revelation gives us the conditions in which the world can exist, that is, in which its preservation is in fact possible. But this preservation is absolutely unrealizable in itself. Even if we bring together all of the logical, physical, political, and economic conditions, even if we bring into being these conditions that God lays out, it counts for nothing if we do not work for this preservation with salvation in mind. For God is not preserving the world on the one hand and saving it on the other. He is preserving it *by* saving it, and he is saving it by using this preservation.[18] The will to preservation and the order of preservation are the same as the will to salvation and the proclamation of the gospel. But this must become incarnate in a real world, and our actions as well as our words must be oriented to the world's present situation, without allowing this situation to change either the content or the unity of this will of God.

The world's will is always a will to death, a will to suicide. This suicide cannot be accepted, and we must act precisely so that it does not occur. We need to know therefore what the present form of the world's will to suicide is, in order to oppose it, to know how and where to direct our efforts. The world is not capable of preserving itself or of finding solutions to its spiritual situation (which governs everything else). The world carries the weight of sin and is the domain of Satan, who is leading it away from God and thus toward death. This is all that it can do. It is not our job then to build the city of God, to raise up an order of God within this world while remaining unconcerned with its tendencies and suicide. Our job is to place ourselves at the very point where this will to suicide is active, in its present form, and see how God's will to preservation can operate there in the given situation. If we do not wish to be completely theoretical, we are thus obliged to understand what our world's mortal tendency is, in depth and in its spiritual reality. This is where we need to apply our effort (and not on the false problems that the world presents, or on an ill-considered application of an order of God that has become abstract). And if we act in this way, we understand that the work of preaching necessarily goes along with the work of material redemption.[19]

18. *Il le conserve* en *le sauvant. Et il le sauve en utilisant cette conservation.* In sentence constructions such as these, the French preposition *en* may be translated into English as *by, in, on,* or *while.* The meaning of *by* seems the most likely here.

19. *Sauvetage,* salvage or rescue.

And so, it is by placing ourselves always at this point of encounter that we Christians can be truly present in the world and perform effective social or political work, by God's grace.

In the chapters that follow, we will attempt to inquire into some of the contemporary manifestations of this will to death, and the Christian's attitude in the face of these realities.

CHAPTER TWO

Revolutionary Christianity

Given our world's situation, everyone feels more or less strongly the need for this civilization to undergo a profound change, a radical transformation. They call this "revolution."[1] On the other hand, people's lives are filled with such motion and uncertainty, such a ferment of ideas, social configurations, and events, that they are quite apt to say that the world is revolutionary already. In fact, they see so many novel solutions being proposed and so many parties calling themselves revolutionary that they have no doubt about this fact: there are more revolutionaries today than ever before in history. The result is that the people of our day are content to remain at this point: they sense that a revolution must occur, and they are convinced that it is occurring already. For this reason, we need to scrutinize more deeply this situation that we are living in.

There is hardly any need to insist that revolution is needed. Our Western civilization has imposed its mechanical and rational mold on the whole world, but it leads to a fatal deadlock. Disaster in all its forms has fallen upon the entire earth as never before. Totalitarian wars, dictatorial empires, administratively organized famines, complete moral breakdown in contexts both social (nation, family) and internal (individual amorality), the fabulous increase in wealth that does not benefit the most destitute, the enslavement of almost all humanity under the domination of states or

---

1. Revolution and revolt receive a great deal of Ellul's attention. See *Autopsy of Revolution*, *De la révolution aux révoltes*, and *Changer de révolution*. (DG)

individuals (capitalism), the depersonalization of humanity as a whole and individually—all this is well known.

Human beings do not really feel at ease in this adventure. They have hardly any security or hope. They demand change, and indeed things must change. But the more they move forward, the more they realize how ineffective human solutions are. These all fail in turn and make our predicament even worse. The more progress we make, the more we prove ourselves incapable of ruling and directing the world that has issued from our hands. Each of us, despite our desire to remain hopeful, is well aware of this. So our thirst grows all the more to see real change occur at last, change that would put everything in its place.

Thus, when we consider that the world is in trouble, cure is impossible, and revolution is needed, we are inclined to say that this world is apocalyptic, that it is the world of the last days. It is easy to respond to this idea ironically and remark that people have always believed their own era to be unique, tragic, and final. There have always been voices to this effect, in the second century, around the year 1000, or in the sixteenth century. Why should our era be more troubled or apocalyptic than any other? It only appears that way. Two hundred years from now, when the details that preoccupy us today have been forgotten, our times will seem just like others, historical rather than apocalyptic. So let us not be led astray by our emotions and illusions.

We must respond to this argument by saying that it is not a question of evaluating objectively whether these times are more or less miserable than those of the past. What matters in our eyes—not the eyes of the historian, but of humankind—is not objective, material "reality" but the idea that we form of it and the suffering and hope and worry of those who live within it. It is not unreasonable for the average person today to feel completely distraught. This is what matters. And besides, as Christians, it is essential to understand that each moment we live through is actually not historical but apocalyptic. If we take the fall seriously, the expulsion from Eden, which entails the constant presence of death—and if we take seriously the promise of Christ's return, of which we know neither the day nor the hour[2]—we must indeed consider the present moment as apocalyptic, which is to say, as the final moment before judgment and pardon. The only vision that Christians can have of the world they live in is an apocalyptic one. Well aware that the present moment may not be the end of the world in the historical

---

2. Matt 24:36; 25:13; Mark 13:32.

sense, they must act as if it were the last. This is the meaning of the counsel often given, "Keep watch!"[3] What counts is not the world's actual end but that life is truly apocalyptic at this very moment. This is the sense in which our world is apocalyptic, but we must not separate it from the demand of all our contemporaries for a revolution [of the kind] that they sense is needed.

* * *

Despite the conviction that our era is revolutionary, we must also recognize that under the appearance of movement and development we are in fact living in complete stasis. There is undoubtedly much chaos and violence, there is technical progress, there are social and political experiments. But in reality our world is static, because its structures remain absolutely fixed and its development unfolds along a completely expected rather than revolutionary path.

There are in fact a certain number of values and forces that are decisive in our world civilization: the primacy of production, the constant increase in the powers of the state and the formation of the nation state, the autonomous rise of technique, and so on. These among others are the elements that make up this world, much more than ownership of the means of production or any totalitarian doctrine.[4] And these elements are static to the very extent to which they are not called into question. All development today consists in advancing the structures of our civilization. All parties, whether revolutionary or conservative, liberal or socialist, on the right or the left, are in accord about preserving these fundamental phenomena.

Besides, how could it be otherwise, seeing the agreement that exists between facts and sentiments—when, for example, technique increases in all areas, and we expect it to provide the greatest benefit. Yet all of the catastrophes that afflict our era are very closely linked to these structures. Long and detailed studies would be necessary to demonstrate this, and that is not our purpose here. While we await such studies, we will limit ourselves to

---

3. Matt 24:42; Mark 13:33–37.

4. Ellul believes that the analysis of Karl Marx was correct for the nineteenth century, but that by the twentieth century, *technique* had become the primary driver of history and society. For Marx, private ownership of the means of production must be abolished and replaced by collective ownership, in order to establish justice and abundance. For liberal economists, private ownership competing in a free market is the key to economic and social progress. For Ellul, technique in all areas of life (not just as means of production) was driving change equally, East or West, liberal or collectivist. (DG)

this assertion: the worldwide catastrophes of the present time are not the result of chance or misfortune, they are not setbacks in the happy outworking of progress. They are the inevitable result of the very structure of our civilization.

It is absolutely useless then to try to find solutions while these structures are left intact. Yet everyone complies with them, as we have said, and in addition they have not yet been understood and revealed in their reality. So it is futile to speak of revolution—or, to be precise, if we do speak of it we should do so according to the new conception that Marxism offers: revolution is not a subversion of the natural course of history; revolution is the acceleration of this natural course.

Thus the revolution that we can anticipate is an ever greater reinforcement of the power of the state, an ever fuller subordination of human beings to their economic function, a more complete disappearance of the person within the mass, and so on. In brief, a reinforcement of the structures! We must not expect such revolution to at all improve the ill effects that we are enduring. Clearly, it has nothing to do with the hope of contemporary people.

What is more, we are indeed obliged to conclude that any other revolution is now impossible. This is because, in order to succeed, it would need to use the very means of today's world. For example, in order to liberate humankind, the compliance of many people would be required; this means that propaganda would have to be in routine use. A politics of the mass would have to be instituted, because that alone can succeed today and it is useless to attempt revolution on some other basis. But if we create a mass, we cooperate precisely with these structures. To free humankind, we would start by destroying everything that still remains free in each person. We would have the equivalent of the "chorus of free people" in *Ubu in Bondage*.[5]

This is the whole tragedy of communism and fascism. They are incapable of producing authentic revolution in our civilization because they adopt the essential facts of this civilization and are content to march along in the direction of these facts' internal development. Using what this world itself offers, they become enslaved to it while claiming to transform it. All of the revolutions that communism and fascism advocate are surface changes that do nothing for the true problem of our time.[6]

5. *Ubu enchaîné*, a satiric play about power by Alfred Jarry (1873–1907).
6. See note 1, p. 103.

This profound stasis, this incapacity for revolution, is certainly the essential characteristic of our era. It stands in opposition to the growing desire to bring this necessary revolution about, and it leads to a society of increasing formlessness. Despite the struggles between parties, which have never been so lively, despite the apparent contradictions, there is a progression toward uniformity, an alignment of all values and ideologies according to several primary structures.

It is not that conflicts don't exist; they do. But they are illusory—which is to say that the people who are struggling do so for illusions.[7] This is not one of the least tragedies at present. Incapable of truly modifying their condition, these people sacrifice themselves for the wrong reasons. The present struggles are not really revolutionary. They are the struggles of individuals and parties; it is a question of knowing who will take power. They are discussions about means (while ends are not called into question); they are oppositions of powers (but not of ways of conceiving the world). Thus communist society is based on the same essential facts as capitalist society, and the USSR obeys the same basic rules as does the USA. People are no freer on one side than on the other; they are just placed into the service of production by different means. They are no more safeguarded on one side than on the other; they are just assimilated into different masses. Justice is flouted as much on the right as on the left, but for different reasons. And so on. Whether a person lives in a dictatorship or a democracy, financial technique is the same everywhere, just as the American rationalization of work is very close to Stakhanovism.[8]

Once the premises of our civilization are accepted, only appearances can change. Individual or state capitalism, Western or Eastern democracy, are like different suits of clothing on the same person. But the habit does not make the monk. Yet it is for this habit that the men and women, indeed even the children, of our time are being called on to kill one other, for the sake of this revolution that they desire but which the very conditions of their struggle prevent them from accomplishing.

7. Ellul's sociology of politics is found in *The Political Illusion*. Many of his other works explore the history of the nation state, the impact of technique or technology on the state and politics, the strategy of anarchism, the theological critique of government and politics, and related topics. (DG)

8. Scientific management or Taylorism in the United States, named for Frederick Taylor (1856–1915), and Stakhanovism in the Soviet Union, named for Aleksei Stakhanov (1906–77), were techniques for making labor more efficient.

* * *

We may well wonder, however, what in general motivates people *at present* to remain blind to the world we are living in. The motive that most powerfully weighs on us like a proscription, the one that keeps us from calling the structures of this civilization into question and embarking on the path of necessary revolution, is undoubtedly our respect for the fact. It is well known that other civilizations did not have the same degree of respect for facts; facts were not viewed in the same way. Today, the fact, whatever it may be—the established fact, the material fact—is the final reason, the criterion of truth. Everything that is a fact is justified by that alone. It is thought that no judgment can be brought to bear on facts; the only thing possible is to bow before them.[9]

And from then on, from the moment that technique, the state, or production are accepted as facts, it seems right to worship them as facts and try to accommodate ourselves to them. Here we have the essence of truly modern religion, the religion of the established fact—the religion that the inferior religions of the dollar, the race, or the proletariat derive from, which are nothing but expressions of the great modern divinity, the Fact-Moloch.[10] And the process is always the same. The fact "proletariat" is taken up, or the fact "state," or the fact "money," and made into a god. It is then imposed on a whole group of people, bluntly and simply, because all modern people in their hearts embrace the worship of the fact. Fact and truth seem to everyone as one and the same. And if God is no longer true today, it is because he does not look like a fact. Thus religion is produced from this feature of the masses' firm conviction. To have a religion, no grand declarations and dogmas, or ceremonies and practices, are needed; all that is required is the support of the crowd's heart. So if we are looking for what the collective worship of our time consists in, it is easy to see that regardless of its form it has to do with the fact. It is enough to leaf through the illustrated newspapers to realize this.

---

9. What have been lost are such things as purpose, human values, revelation, community, tradition, paradox, and mystery. *Facts* are disconnected, measurable phenomena that are available to our senses. They come at us in a blizzard of "factoids" and bits. We survey them, count them, and call them "established facts," and believe them to be reality. (DG)

10. Moloch or Molech, an ancient Near Eastern god that was propitiated by child sacrifice. The name symbolizes that which demands extreme sacrifice.

Those who question the value of the fact incur the harshest of all reproaches today: they are reactionaries, they want to return to the good old days, and so on. . . . Those who level this reproach do not realize that such doubt is perhaps the sole revolutionary attitude that is currently possible. Even so, we need to know the reason why we refuse to bow before the fact, for the surrealistic approach does not seem desirable.

The atomic bomb provides quite a striking example of this religious authority that the fact carries. In the face of this discovery, this instrument of death, humankind retained the possibility of not using it, of not accepting this fact. But this question was not even posed. We found ourselves before a fact; thus we had to accept it. And from that point on, the questions asked were "secondary." Who will use this weapon? How will its control be arranged? What will be most expedient: to use nuclear power for war, or for peace? How can the economy be organized around nuclear power? and so forth, and so on. At no time was the problem posed of knowing if it was good or evil to embark on this path, and this was because the fact today seems to be beyond good and evil.

So the questions that throng around a phenomenon like that of the atomic bomb are questions that arise from things, from the fact—and that are imposed on humankind. They are not questions that humankind poses to itself, or imposes on matter. It is the atomic bomb that forces people to think and become agitated and look for answers. The problems prompted by the existence of the bomb are what seem greatest, which is to say, problems that are imposed by a fact. They are no longer questions that human beings, "because they know good and evil,"[11] can pose about the very existence of the atomic bomb, the existence of a fact. Thus human beings divest themselves of their true superiority, and those who claimed to dominate things as well as the world now make themselves the slaves of facts, in a way that no dictatorship of the mind had ever dared hope was possible! Having wanted to be master of material forces, human beings now place themselves in subjection to base matter, expressed through the fact. Now thought, life, feelings, everything submits to experimental control, to fact.

Now, what seems important for our purpose is that this submission to the fact is the anti-revolutionary position *par excellence*. Between Creon and Antigone, modern people can countenance only Creon.[12] To the extent

---

11. Gen 3:5, 22.

12. Antigone defied King Creon's order not to bury her brother's body. The most well-known expression of this story is found in Sophocles' play *Antigone* (fifth century BC).

that the revolutionary act enters into conflict with the power of the fact, it is desperate. But modern people no longer enter into conflict with facts.

Proudhon was revolutionary, because he affirmed the supremacy of the human will over the human condition and called people to struggle against their situation.[13] Marx, by contrast, taught that socialist society would emerge inevitably from capitalist society through the development of facts[14] (including this simple fact that human beings are[15]) and through the interplay of historical dialectic. Marx was therefore anti-revolutionary. As socialism has become scientific, which is to say, as it has subjected itself to the fact and followed the outworking of facts, it has become anti-revolutionary. The worship of the fact requires human beings to subordinate their will to the way in which the facts unfold. This is so much the case that today whenever opposition to a fact becomes evident, it is because its opponent has concluded that the situation would change and a new state of fact would arrive. The fact of the future is preferred to the fact that is currently on the way out. But this is the affirmation of an outcome, not of a truth.

For as long as society has existed, the revolutionary spirit has been a necessary part of social life. It has always meant the affirmation of a truth of a spiritual order over against the error of the moment. Such truth must become incarnate in society, not by an automatic mechanism, but by the desperate effort of human beings, by their sacrifice. They do this because of a hope that is greater than they and by the power of their freedom to resist all necessities and conformisms. This is the permanent essence of revolutions. We refuse to give this term another meaning. Revolution is not the course of history. It can divert history, it can push it back, but in no way does revolution simply follow along in history's wake. There is a natural course to history, and revolution consists in rising up against this natural (or dialectical) course, in the name of a truth and a freedom that are endangered by "normal" development. If the revolution succeeds, people will say afterward, "That was evidently the true course of history!" But this is a historian's illusion. The [possible] combinations of social, political, and economic facts are infinite at any given moment, and [one particular] outcome

---

For Ellul's purpose here, Creon symbolizes power, and Antigone symbolizes resistance to that power.

13. Pierre-Joseph Proudhon (1809–65), theorist of anarchism.

14. The French noun *fait* may be translated as *fact* or *event*. For consistency, *fait* is translated as *fact* throughout this translation.

15. *Y compris ce simple fait qu'est l'homme*, including this simple fact that is man. The precise meaning is unclear.

is never a rigorous necessity. Our choices are what give the preponderance to one outcome, which is just as valid as the others (but no more so!). And this choice can be conformist, in the sense of that which is normally predictable with the general line of development—or it can be revolutionary, in the sense of [revealing] a new truth, one that is yet unknown as a social force.

So people today who espouse political and economic liberalism, the capitalist system, and classical democracy are advocating for the fact of today. They do so without contemplating that the fact of today rises and falls. History is irreversible. Their position amounts to conformity to the past. Those who espouse socialism (and principally in its extreme forms, Nazism and communism) have for the last century taken the prevailing course as their reference point and have tended to follow along in its direction. They are just as much conformists, but conformists of the future. And if these doctrines have much success, it is because the mass is conformist by nature.

The revolutionary position is something other. But it is still to be determined, because it cannot be merely the affirmation of truth or freedom (which ones?)—or the affirmation of some new political doctrine. A revolutionary position is total. We must understand, then, that if this revolution does not occur, the chips are down and no human civilization is possible. We stand now before a choice. Either we will have the civilization of the mass, technological, conformist, Huxley's "best of all possible worlds," hell organized on earth for the physiological happiness of all[16]—or we will have another civilization, one that we cannot describe in advance because it must be made by conscious beings. If we do not know how to choose, which means, precisely, if we do not know how to effect revolution, if we let ourselves be carried along by the current of history, we will have chosen, without knowing it, in favor of the power of suicide that lies at the world's heart. But we can hardly have any illusions. Faced with the power of how

16. The novel *Brave New World* by Aldous Huxley (1894–1963) is known in French translation as *Le Meilleur des mondes* (The Best of [All Possible] Worlds). Both titles refer to expressions of naive praise for humanity, found respectively in Shakespeare's *Tempest* and Voltaire's *Candide*. The phrase *meilleur des mondes* comes originally from the *Théodicée* (Theodicy) of Gottfried Leibniz (1646–1716). According to Alfred A. Knopf, Huxley was instrumental to the decision to publish Ellul's *La Technique* in English translation, which brought Ellul to prominence in North America. Huxley was "asked his opinion about contemporary European works on the subject [of technology]. Huxley recommended above all Ellul's *La Technique*, which had been published in Paris by Armand Colin in 1954 without having attracted much attention." (See "Statement from the Publisher" in Ellul, *The Technological Society*.)

things are organized, our revolutionary consciousness is almost impotent. And besides, we do not see, in the world, which people have a revolutionary consciousness.

2

Christians' situation in the world is a revolutionary one. They contribute to the world's preservation by being, in the world's midst, a revolutionary and inexhaustible power. It is indeed a matter of the world's preservation. For in our time, as I have tried to demonstrate above, "to go along with history" leads to catastrophe, the death of many men, women, and children (as we have seen!), the extinction of possibility for human civilization, and the technical establishment of suicide. For the world to be preserved, an authentic revolution must take place today.

But when we say that the Christian situation is revolutionary and the possible source of our civilization's transformation, this appears to be a paradox and a counter-truth. Revolutionary Christians have not always been apparent throughout history, and certainly not at the present time. Today it seems quite certain that Christians are the most conformist, most docile of all people. What is more, theologians seem anti-revolutionary by necessity, because they teach respect toward the authorities and that all authority comes from God.[17] But the fact that during certain periods Christians lose sight of the revolutionary implications of their faith does not mean therefore that the Holy Spirit ceases to be at work, or that Christians' situation ceases to be revolutionary to the extent that they confess their faith within the world.

The Holy Spirit's intervention, and the revolutionary nature of the Christian situation, do not depend on us and on our choices. The reason that some people become Christians is not that they choose Christ, but that Christ has chosen them. Some Christians work in the world not because they choose to go there, but because Christ sends them. They are revolutionary not because they feel the urgency for revolution, but for another reason entirely, which we will need to examine later. That the Christian situation is revolutionary is not due to a stance of the human mind or will. It is so by necessity, and it cannot be otherwise insofar as Christ is acting in his church. This situation is one of the church's works within the world. And besides, it is quite true (I do not mean this as a proof, but as a simple

17. Rom 13:1.

observation) that throughout most of its history, the church has indeed been in a revolutionary situation.

But we still need to clarify: we are referring to a situation, not necessarily to an activity. It is in short a state of permanent revolution. It can be translated into a concerted action, but it can also remain in a state of fermentation and lead to a gradual but deeply penetrating work. Such work is just as revolutionary as an abrupt and obvious upheaval. Upheaval is an end stage or crisis, but not revolution's whole.

It is also a revolution with regard to the world and not only with regard to the state or the government. One can be conformist toward the government and yet revolutionary toward the world. The idea of revolution goes deeper here; it does not essentially have to do with changing a form of the state or an economic form but precisely with changing a civilization's structures, which must constantly be called into question. Clearly, such a change will indirectly produce deep governmental or economic changes. But it does not necessarily lead to direct conflict with authority, unless that authority defends the established disorder and openly challenges God's truth of a new order.

We now have a deeper, though preliminary, understanding of what this revolutionary character of the Christian faith can be in today's world. We must now investigate the conditions and implications of this situation.

* * *

The first condition is a well-known truth, but not sufficiently understood in its reality: *Christians belong to two cities.* They are in the world. They have a social life. They are citizens of a nation, belong to a family, and are employed and must work to earn money. They lead their lives in the context of other people and in their company. They share the same nature and condition. All that they do in this world they must do seriously, because they are joined with others. They cannot neglect what are called "duties,"[18] because they are human beings like others. But, on the other hand, they cannot belong entirely to this world. For them it is always just a temporary "tent" (2 Pet 1:13)[19] in which they are "strangers and sojourners" (Heb 11:13). For them the situation is provisional, although extremely important, because

18. Likely a reference to *devoirs d'état*, duties or obligations that arise from one's estate (situation) in society, as described in the catechism of Pope Pius X (1835–1914).

19. See also 2 Cor 5:1.

they belong to another city. They take their belonging[20] and their thinking from elsewhere. They have another Lord.

And this must be taken in the most rigorously material sense. In this world, they belong to another world. They are like people of a particular nation who reside in a foreign country. Chinese people living in France think according to their own concepts and traditions and have their own criteria for judgment and action. They are truly foreigners while also citizens of another state. Their allegiance is directed toward that state and not toward their country of residence.[21] Thus it is with Christians. They are citizens of another kingdom, and they draw their ways of thinking, judging, and feeling from there. Their heart and mind lie elsewhere. They are subjects of another state and are its ambassadors on earth (2 Cor 5:20). This means that they must present their Lord's demands and establish a relation between the two [realms]. But they cannot adopt this world's interests; they defend their Lord's interests, just as ambassadors defend the interests of their state.

Viewed in another way, they can also be sent as spies. This may in fact be the Christian's situation: to work secretly in the heart of the world on the Lord's behalf, preparing the Lord's victory from within. They can infiltrate this world and expose its secrets, creating the conditions for the kingdom of God to burst forth. Just like the spies sent into the country of Canaan (Josh 2:1; Heb 11:30).

Regardless of their particular situation in the world, their ties are elsewhere, ties of thinking, truth, and loyalty. All these depend on the Lord, and they owe no loyalty to the world. Besides, when we speak of this world, it implies certain concrete realities: nation, state, family, work. . . . Christians cannot pledge unconditional loyalty to any of these. Their first loyalty is to their Lord (Matt 10:37).[22]

Now, the two cities in which Christians are involved can never coincide, yet they cannot abandon either one or the other. They may long to return through death to their city of origin, their homeland, but as long as they are on the earth there is no way that they can renounce either one. But neither can they be satisfied with the fundamental duality that they are caught up in. In other terms, the contradiction that is in their heart, this tension that we were describing in chapter one, reappears here, but

---

20. *Filiation*, sonship, descent.

21. Clearly, Ellul is referring to Chinese people who are temporarily resident in France, not to Chinese immigrants who wish to become French citizens.

22. See note 2, p. 105.

transcribed into social, political, and economic reality. Christians bound up with this world's material history are involved as representatives of another order, another Lord (than the prince of this world), another claim (than that of the natural heart). Thus they must first accept this tension, this opposition, and that results from accepting their internal tension—because they know that the two realms are irreconcilable. They must accept that the opposition between this world and the kingdom of God is total.

But this is an intolerable situation. It means keen suffering and is not satisfying to recognize. Christians can never consider themselves as on the right side, looking contentedly upon the perdition of everything else; to do so is to fail the charity of Christ and cease in this way even to be Christians. Being joined with others (through economic, sociological, and other such laws, and also by God's will), they cannot agree to watch them trapped in their distress and dissolution, handed over to tyranny, unceasing labor, and unfounded hope. They need to immerse themselves in social and political problems so that they can act in the world, not in the hope of making it a paradise, but only of rendering it tolerable. Not of attenuating the opposition between this world and the kingdom of God, but only the opposition between this world's disorder and the order of preservation that God wants for it. Not of making the kingdom of God come, but so that the gospel may be proclaimed, that all people may hear *truly* the good news of salvation and resurrection.

So we have three directions in which Christians must act in the world.[23] First, beginning with what God reveals to them about the human person, they must seek out the social and political conditions in which such persons can live and develop as God has commanded them to do. Next, [they must recognize that] these persons develop in a certain setting that God has placed them in, which is the order of preservation, without which human beings lack their true milieu of life. They are not completely free in this sphere any more than they are in the physical or biological sphere. There are certain limits that they cannot overstep without causing the society that they live in to be destroyed. So Christians must strive so that the order that God desires can be embodied in particular, existing institutions and organizations. Third, this order of preservation has meaning only if it is oriented toward the proclamation of salvation. Social and political

---

23. Note that Ellul is here outlining a strategic direction. When he writes that he will not do so, or that we cannot do so, he means to emphasize that there can be no abstract, unchangeable formula for faithful action in the world. (DG)

institutions therefore need to be "open," they cannot claim to be complete, absolute—they must be constituted in such a way that they do not prevent people from hearing the Word of God. Christians must see to this also, insightfully and without compromise.

But in doing this, they find themselves before two possible errors. One consists in believing that by a constant progress in this order, the kingdom of God will be attained; a reference to the book of Revelation or to Matthew 24 is all that it takes to put an end to such thinking. The other error would result from the belief that if particular reforms were effected, this order that God desires would come about. In reality, all solutions, all economic, political, and other achievements, are temporary. Christians cannot at any time or to any extent believe that they are complete and will endure. They are always contaminated by the sin that binds them, by the very environment in which they exist.

Thus Christians are constantly obliged to renew God's demand, to bring this order repeatedly into confrontation with an order that is moving constantly toward disorder. And because of God's always-fresh demand on the world, Christians are placed in this way in a permanently revolutionary situation. Even when the institutions, laws, and reforms that they advocate come to pass, even if society is reorganized along the lines that they have advocated, they must remain in opposition and require yet more, because what God demands is infinite, as is his pardon. Thus Christians are called to continually question all that is termed progress, discoveries, facts, established results, reality, and so on. They cannot be satisfied at any time with all this toil, and, as a result, they must demand that it be surpassed and replaced.

They exercise their judgment according to the Spirit—they do what is essentially revolutionary. If it is not so, it is because in some way Christians have betrayed their vocation in the world.

* * *

We have just seen one of the elements that make this condition necessary, and it is Christians' very situation in the world. But there is a second fact, yet more significant if that be possible, which is the promise of the glorious return of Jesus Christ—the *parousia*.[24] Christians are essentially people

24. A Greek noun meaning *presence, appearing,* or *coming* and typically used in the New Testament in reference to the second coming of Christ. See for example Matt 24.

who live in expectation.[25] [It is the] expectation of the Lord's return, which accompanies the end of time, the judgment, and which announces the kingdom of God. So those who know they are saved by Christ are not people attached jealously or fearfully to a past, however glorious it may be, not the past of their church (the tradition) or even the past life of Jesus Christ (who does, however, support and uphold the assurance of their faith). They are instead people of the future, and not of a temporal and natural future, but of the *eschaton*,[26] the future break with this present world. They are thus cast forward, propelled toward this moment, and for them all facts take their value from the kingdom of God that is coming, from the judgment and triumph of the Lord. This is true for all theological facts. Just as the entire Old Testament is able to take its full meaning, *as the work of God*, only from the person of Christ, so also the life of Christ. All his preaching takes its meaning from the cross, and the cross has value only in the resurrection, and the resurrection itself is made clear only by the ascension (this declaration that Christ is Lord). But let us not get into a theological discussion!

This theological truth also applies, however, to social and political facts. The current events of our world take their value only from the perspective of the kingdom of God that is coming. The imminence of Christ's return is what gives an authentic seriousness to each news item; current affairs receive their genuine content from it. Without this direction, history is an explosion of insanity. Now, the function of Christians in this regard is not to be content with this knowledge but to make this coming event present in the world now, through their action and thought. They bear in the present day the elements of the *eschaton*. They fill thereby a prophetic function. And as the historians have noted, the prophets of Israel always had a political role that, in relation to their civilization, was authentically revolutionary. All Christians having received the Holy Spirit are now prophets of Christ's return, and by this alone they have a revolutionary mission in politics. For prophets do not merely announce to some extent an event that will happen at some point. Prophets are those who live out the event now and who make it real and present to the world around them.[27]

25. The whole Bible seems to look forward in hope to God's future intervention in human history, and even to a great end (in Greek, *eschaton*). And more than just a forward look and expectation, there is a behavior associated with it: "The night is far gone, the day is near. . . . Let us live as in the day . . ." (Rom 13:12–13). (DG)

26. A Greek noun meaning *end* and used in the New Testament primarily in reference to the *end of time*. See for example John 6:39–40.

27. Ellul describes the role of the prophet in his commentary on 2 Kings, *The Politics*

Now, such is indeed the revolutionary situation: to be revolutionary is to pass judgment on what is, on actual facts, in the name of a truth that is not yet (but is to come). And it means doing so in the belief that this truth is more authentic, more real, than the reality that surrounds us. As a result, it means causing the future to intervene as an explosive power in the present, believing that future events are more important and true than present ones, and coming to understand and grasp the present by way of the future, governing it by the future in the same way that the historian stands over the past. And the revolutionary act will then participate in history. It will create history by bending it toward this future. This concept of revolution is valid for all of the revolutions that have occurred over the course of history, whether they succeeded or not. It is also true of the communist movement—but it destroyed its revolutionary power itself, as we have seen, in favor of the natural course as the greatest inclination of history. To act for the future fact that is *most likely* and brought on by present circumstances is actually to no longer act in a revolutionary manner.

Christians, by contrast, even without engaging in great political speeches or demonstrations of revolutionary power, but by living truly in the power of Christ and making actual through hope the coming of the kingdom, are in the most revolutionary situation possible. They judge the present time by virtue of a meta-historical fact. This fact's intervention in the present time is the only thing capable of freeing civilization from the suffocating social and political structures under which it is slowly weakening and dying. And here again, it is not a question of representing this to ourselves as an optional capacity, as one attitude among others. It is the only attitude of faith that is possible. To desert this situation is in reality to cease believing that we are saved—for we are saved by hope, through faith (Rom 8:24), and hope is precisely this power of eschatology in the present.

Thus we grasp the two theological roots that make the Christian life necessarily revolutionary—roots that are not created by each person's will but by the situation in which God places his children. We must be

---

of God and the Politics of Man, 20–21, 50. "Man chooses his own action. But between this decision by man and God's decision we find the prophet. This man has received a revelation of God's intention. . . . He announces and can bend or provoke, but there is no necessity or determination. One is in the presence of open possibilities here. The man also understands what the politician is wanting. He understands it in depth. He sees the reality behind the appearance of the action and he discloses to the politician his true intention, his situation. Finally, this man gives the meaning of it all, the true significance of what has happened. . . . The prophet is in effect the man who brings a Word of God to bear on the actual, concrete situation of man, his political situation." (DG)

persuaded that if we do not live in the light of this vision, we are completely uninformed of what the Christian life is all about. There are still more conclusions to draw from this.

* * *

A first order of conclusions will likely appear even more abstract and difficult! It is that Christians must not judge, act, or live according to principles, but according to the reality of the *eschaton*, lived out here and now. This is exactly the opposite of a moralism.

We need to be convinced that there are no Christian principles.[28] There is the person of Christ, who is the principle of all things,[29] but if we want to be faithful there can be no question of reducing Christianity (as too often has happened) to a certain number of principles from which implications could be straightforwardly derived. This act of transforming the work of the living God into a philosophical doctrine is the constant temptation and greatest betrayal of theologians—and also of the faithful, when they transform the action of the Spirit, who causes his fruits to be born in them, into a moral system, a new law, a set of principles to apply. The Christian life does not result from a cause but is directed toward an end. This is what changes human perspectives completely and makes the Christian life unique from any other.

What is true on the individual level is true also on the social. There are no political and social Christian principles that can be defined in an absolute way. What God reveals to us in this area through Scripture is not a doctrine or principles, but judgments and action that are entirely focused on accomplishing God's work. We never observe a straight or causal course any more than we see a static and more-or-less permanent order established. God's action always appears as a power in motion, as a torrent that crosses and re-crosses history, that *changes course*,[30] rolls in waves, and

---

28. What Ellul means is that there are no abstract, stand-alone principles. We follow a Commander, not a set of abstract commands. There will be guidance, and it will be consistent with the character of God, not chaotic, not at all the whim of human interest and desire. But God is alive, and our situations always have novel aspects, and we are unique individuals. No stand-alone system of principles and rules can ever be allowed to threaten or replace that existential reality. (DG)

29. Col 1:15–18.

30. *Qui change ses bords*, that changes its banks. The meaning is unclear, but perhaps refers to a current that moves from one side of the river to the other.

33

churns up all the particles of creation. Scripture shows us a God at work in political and civil history, using the works of human beings and sweeping them along in his action toward the kingdom that he has promised.

From what Scripture reveals to us about this activity, we can draw some analogous conclusions. We can conceive of some main themes by which our action can be oriented. We can glimpse the outlines of an order that is in current motion, but not a system or political principles. When it is a matter of transcribing God's action in the world, in an incomplete and humanly intelligible way, there can be no question of any dogmatism whatever. That is the very opposite of this action.

Thus, the first implication of this revolutionary function of Christians is that they should be open to all human action, accepting it as a [potentially] valid orientation. We can never rule out a political or social endeavor because of supposed Christian principles. Everything that appears to be a step in the direction that we have laid out above should be taken up for examination and, of course, questioned thoroughly.[31]

But it is clear that Christians can never consider themselves tied to the past or to a principle. In the political world they must apply the rule of Ecclesiastes 3: "There is a time for everything. . . . God has made each thing good in its time." There is no Christian standpoint that is valid for all times. Positions that seem contradictory can be equally sound, depending on the times, insofar as they express in history a faithfulness to God's design. So they must not maintain loyalty to an idea, doctrine, or political outcome. What the world calls loyalty is usually habit or obstinacy. Christians can move right or left, can be liberal or socialist, according to the circumstances and the position that seems more conformed to God's will *at this time*. These positions are contradictory, it is true, from the human point of view. They must draw their unity from pursuing the kingdom that is to come. Christians are called to judge the present circumstances in light of this kingdom. These circumstances cannot be judged by their particular moral or political content, any more than by their relation to a human doctrine or their attachment to the past, but simply by their always-existing relation to the *parousia*. This is a difficult position, full of pitfalls and dangers, but it is also the only one that appears true to the Christian life. And we have never been told that the Christian life should be easy or secure.

31. In his *Violence: Reflections from a Christian Perspective*, Ellul is unequivocal that violence is one form of action that can never be Christian. If we participate in any violence, we must not attempt to justify it as Christian. This is certainly a "principle"—but Ellul doesn't want it detached from a relationship with the living Prince of Peace. (DG)

The fact that almost all Christian political stances have been mistaken or catastrophic (that of the Jesuits as much as of Constantine, for example)[32] is because the kingdom has been deliberately replaced by a moral doctrine as the basis for judgment and because efforts have always been made to "derive a politics from the gospel!"[33]

But, it will be asked, what do we know of this kingdom of God? In reality, we need to guard against turning the kingdom of God into a moral system that we could reduce to simple rules and replicate on earth! The central point that we already know and is already actual is the Lordship of Jesus Christ, and that it is on this Lordship that the whole of Christian realism must be founded. This actual Lordship is the objective element in the revolutionary Christian situation, as hope is its subjective element. And this alone is what enables us to orient ourselves in our various political positions and successive judgments about the concrete problems of politics and the economy.

A thing is never good or bad in itself, not even by the use that human beings make of it (according to a mistaken but quite widespread formula!). A thing is good or bad only in the time in which it is, according to its situation from the perspective of God's kingdom, its conformity with God's work for the coming of the kingdom, and, finally, whether it can or cannot be used for God's glory. These are three criteria, as precise and practical as can be, [that emerge] when we cease being obsessed with moral formulas or political doctrines. It is by daily applying these three criteria to social facts that the activity of Christians is revolutionary in bringing about the *eschaton*.

It is easy to see that this attitude goes far beyond both the idealisms and the realisms of today. The constant presence of the kingdom in the Christian life is a demand that urges us continually to go further, see situations in depth, and make more comprehensive demands, because no revolution can fully satisfy. Likewise, anything that is accomplished, no matter how humble, deserves protection. So we need to take all of the facts into account as well as truly transcend them—and not by some kind of

32. The Jesuits, or Society of Jesus, a religious order established by Ignatius of Loyola (1491–1556) that sought to influence highly placed persons in church, state, and society. Constantine (c. 288–337), a Roman emperor who converted to Christianity, prohibited the state persecution of Christians, and convoked the Council of Nicaea.

33. A reference to *La Politique tirée des propres paroles de l'Écriture sainte* (Politics Drawn from the Very Words of Holy Scripture) by Jacques-Bénigne Bossuet (1627–1704), which used biblical texts to support its political argument.

intellectual contempt or abstract dogmatism. What motivates this realism is that Christians do not follow the criteria of efficiency or success, as other types of realism do, but the Lordship of Christ. Thus they are called to judge all things (1 Thess 5:21), a command that Paul gives absolutely, which is to say, involving all areas of life and not only "moral values" or the spiritual life. It is also fitting to point out that this command appears in this text between the exhortation about prophecies (Do not quench the Spirit, do not despise prophecies) and the reminder that any Christian life has only one goal: to preserve [the world] for the coming of our Lord Jesus Christ (v. 23). Consequently, this sequence lies quite neatly at the heart of all that we have been able to write here about Christians' revolutionary position.

This judgment, which cannot be exercised according to human rules or conventions, but which must always be fresh and new, is the very crux of Christians' realist position. I am quite familiar with the possible criticisms: how much this will seem like a lack of unity, continuity, faithfulness, and so on. But I believe that all of this is the result of a false Christian position, similar to what pagans imagine this position must be. Nothing is more irksome than anti-Christians using biblical texts, which they do not understand, to criticize Christians' positions. The value of their criticism toward Christians does not come from their scriptural skill but from the conduct of their life. Non-Christians are an example to Christians by living in ways that are different and better on a given point (Luke 16:8). But when it comes to advice and teachings on moral and intellectual matters, Christians are not obliged to follow what non-Christians may want to offer them. We can observe Christian thinking and morality aligning [with non-Christian] in this way for the past two centuries. It is the secularization of Christianity by Christians themselves, through their lack of courage and faithfulness. And on this particular point, the criticisms that are addressed to Christian realism manifest this attitude.

* * *

But this realism is not limited to everyday facts. The primary question is posed, as we have seen, by the phenomenon of our civilization's deep structures. These are what condition the catastrophes that we live in, and also what proscribe all revolution. The Christian situation is revolutionary by essence, as we have said, and must be expressed in current facts. It is true that the faithful of the churches no longer have any awareness whatsoever of this situation. They concern themselves as little as possible with what nonetheless constitutes their mission on earth. This is due to various reasons that we cannot examine here. It is also true that the churches have shown themselves as deplorable ambassadors, not knowing how to play this revolutionary part, this role of fermentation or leaven that has been their calling. They have been bogged down in the lowest politics or the highest "spirituality."

But whether we will or not, those who confess Jesus Christ find themselves nonetheless one day brought face to face with this responsibility. They are led to a decision which testifies that their basic situation is a revolutionary one. Whether this decision is conscious or not, it is no less revolutionary. In our day, it is revolutionary because it is the decision of people acting for personal reasons and not for sociological ones. Today this does not often happen.[34]

If we have been led to study this problem, it is not with the conceit of introducing anything new. I believe that I am simply describing here what has always been Christians' situation in the world. If we have been led to realize it, this is not an "advance." It is even, I think, an opposite sign. In reality, it shows that the current problem of revolution is a life-or-death problem for humanity, presented in terms that have never been known before. For no one, unless they are prompted by an "extraterrestrial" power, can claim today to be truly revolutionary. All that belongs to the world has become radically conservative in relation to the powers that relentlessly conduct us toward suicide. On the other hand, and at the same time, Christians no longer act according to this unconscious impulse that has made them, at all times in which the church was alive, the bearers of a profound revolution. It seems that this power today is basically dead in the depths of their hearts—and despite their faith, Christians act mostly as sociological beings. They no longer seem to understand Christian freedom. Therefore, since they are no longer unconscious revolutionaries, they must become conscious ones—at the same time that they must become conscious of their particular mission and their revolutionary calling. If they are no longer so, perhaps because they no longer receive the necessary powers of the Spirit, they must ask God to grant them these powers. They must make them the

---

34. The only true and authentic revolution today is that of the individual against mass society. See "The Necessary Revolution," chapter five of *Autopsy of Revolution*, 233–67. (DG)

object of their prayer, so that they can regain this possibility for action that God opens to them and that is essential for them today.

This revolutionary power, manifested in everyday realism, must also tackle the fundamental questions of our time. It must be applied to changing the fundamental structures (which have nothing to do with what is currently called "structures," which is to say, economic *forms*). It must go much further than our certified revolutionaries in the political parties, who seek only to firmly establish a world that is too well known and nonetheless outdated. How can it do this? It is a long effort. The first [step] is understanding, becoming aware of the world we live in and do not know (because it cannot be said that the world is understood by statistics and opinion polls!).

The next [step involves] a *way of living*. Christians must pursue a way of life that does not differentiate them from others but enables them to elude the influence of structures. The desired results cannot be achieved by attacking the structures directly, trying to make spectacular modifications, or striving to reconstruct a world from their every fragment. The only effective attack against the structures is to succeed in evading them and living on the margin of this totalitarian society, not by rejecting it outright, but by sifting it thoroughly.

In the end, it could be that in communities that hold to a way of living of this order, the *seeds of a new civilization* may spring up. At present, it is not for us to be concerned yet with this eventuality or to distract ourselves with enticing vistas. The first step to take is to become aware[35] of our world, or, to say it another way, to take up a revolutionary stance.[36] If this first step is not taken, everything else is utopian and it is perfectly useless for Christians to concern themselves with social or political questions. Although it seems like an intellectual or spiritual process (that is not all it is, in fact!), it is an extremely difficult decision to make—this decision to break with the ways of the present age. What we are concerned to discover, then, is whether Christians will be bold enough to risk everything in this accomplishment of their function.

---

35. *Prise de conscience*, to become aware in an active and moral sense, in a way that produces an important and irreversible change in one's understanding.

36. *Une mise en situation révolutionnaire*, an entry into a revolutionary situation or state of being.

CHAPTER THREE

End and Means

When we think about the possibilities for action in the world, regardless of the form this action takes (evangelism, for example, or political action), when we arrive at the idea that one's way of living is today one of the surest forms of revolutionary action, and when, thirdly, we seek out ways in which the Christian's faith can be expressed, we are posing the problem of end and means. At the same time, if we consider the present day we quickly note that this is a phrase that preoccupies our contemporaries, directly or indirectly. Intellectuals such as Huxley take up the question directly and in its consequences. [Those who are] not intellectuals take a pragmatic approach that renders it implicit. In reality, the question is absolutely central to our civilization, and the answer provided may be the decisive element in our civilization's decline.

Thus, with "end and means" we are concerned both with the consequences of the preceding study and with the world's activity, which is today significant.[1]

---

1. In this chapter Ellul outlines the heart of the challenge of technology and, more precisely, the *technique* at its core. His most famous and best-selling book is *The Technological Society*, to which he later added *The Technological System* and *The Technological Bluff*. (DG)

1

A first observation is of singular importance: the problem of end and means is an old problem, but it is no longer being presented in the same manner. Today, if we want to study the question from a philosophic angle, either morally or metaphysically, presenting and responding to it in eternal terms, we are condemned to understand nothing about it, although we may seem clever. In reality, today the problem is radically transformed. It is no longer a discussion about two ways of viewing the relationship between end and means (for example, "the end justifies the means" and "the right means for the right ends"). This is because the terms in which the question is being presented are no longer philosophical but empirical. They concern particular facts—and, what is most constraining, technical facts. So this question is indeed key to our times, in the sense that we need to pose it correctly in order to understand our civilization. But posing it correctly means conceiving it as a real fact, which has changed the very nature of the situation. And this fact is technique.

Besides, supplying an abstract answer to the question is not adequate. This would only produce an "ought" that cannot be applied to life. In reality, like most questions of fact that our civilization raises, this one does not call for an intellectual or technical response. It calls those affected to take up sides; it calls for a life decision on the part of those to whom the question is posed. The move is no longer "from abstract question to abstract response," as in some other civilizations, but "from a concrete question to a life position." Those who construct our economic and political systems err when they make them a case of "from concrete question to abstract answer!"

How then is this question of end and means currently being presented? What are its aspects? The first enormous fact that emerges from our civilization is that today everything has become means. The end no longer exists. We no longer know where we are heading. We have forgotten our common purposes, we have enormous means at our disposal, and we put into operation prodigious machines in order to arrive nowhere. The end (and by this I mean our civilization's common end, since individual people still have individual ends, such as winning a competition, receiving a salary increase, and so on) has been effaced before the means. Human beings who were originally the end of this whole humanist system of means, who are still proclaimed as "end" in political speeches, in reality have entirely become means, and a means of these very means that were supposed to serve them, such as the economy or the state. In order for the economy to function well, human beings must submit to the demands of the economic mechanism. As total producers, they place all their efforts into the service of production. As obedient consumers, they swallow blindly all that the economy feeds to them, and so on. Thus, humanity is transformed into an instrument of these modern gods that are our means, and we do it with the good intention of making humanity happy.

In every field the same path has been followed. Here is an example. People must be made happy, and to produce this happiness they must be given many goods to consume. For this, considerable production must be arranged, and consumption must be adjusted to production. But there are human and technical obstacles that make this complicated. The technical ones are progressively overcome through research; the human ones must be overcome by submitting human beings to the machine, the division of labor, advertising, the unlimited use of their energies, and so on. In this way, real, living people, regular people, are placed in submission to means that must assure happiness to "people" in the abstract. The "person" of the philosophers and politicians, which does not exist, is the sole end of this prodigious adventure that produces misery for all people of flesh and blood and transforms them into means.

This process occurs everywhere. Science and technique provide us with another example. Once, knowledge of truth was what mattered, but then after the philosophers came the scientists. They developed their theories, which were then applied, first in order to prove the truth of these theories, and then because of their usefulness. From that point on, science was lost! Technical means gradually came to dominate the search for truth. Science became more and more about the effectiveness of technical means. Science today takes its meaning from technique; it is completely oriented to application. It is in the service of means. It has become a means of perfecting the means. The abstraction "science," to which we still pay lip service, has replaced the search for truth.

Thus we easily perceive that this world is totally delivered over to means. What had been an end a century ago has now become in its turn a means, and even a means of other means! But we retain a mental picture or representation of it [that former end], because the severity of this situation is hard to accept. So we push the ends that we are pursuing into the realm of the ideal, the abstract, the utopian. Communism provides an excellent example in political life. It set in motion the most remarkable doctrine of political means there is. It is more complete than any other. But for what end? "For communist society," will likely be the reply. But "it never occurred to any socialist to promise the coming of the higher stage of communism," Lenin said, adding about this communist society that "no one ever promised it or even planned to institute it, because, generally speaking, it is impossible to institute" (Lenin, *State and Revolution*, chapter 5, §4).[2] Thus we have an admirable political machine that perpetuates itself by means (because the dictatorship of the proletariat is also a means), with a view to illusory and hypothetical ends. And to produce the happiness of future people, those of the present day are sacrificed.

This remarkable proliferation of means therefore leads to everything becoming servile. In our world everything must serve, which is to say, exist as means. Art and all that was formerly "useless" or "gratuitous" must submit to the necessity of "usefulness."[3] Whatever does not serve some purpose must be rejected or eliminated. This very same calculation is applied to human beings. It explains the practice of euthanasia in the National Socialist[4] state toward the elderly and incurable. Whoever serves no purpose to the community must be put to death. This practice seems barbaric to us, but it is simply the application of the universal predominance of means. And to the extent that this fact spreads, we must expect this practice to be introduced through all civilization. It will also be justified by [the argument that it produces] the greatest good and benefit to "humanity."

Besides, as means increase, as ends are pushed into the abstract, ends become implicit and are no longer called into question. Everyone today knows "more or less" the purpose that civilization pursues, and it seems completely pointless and outdated to pose ourselves the question. Everyone has some vague ideas about progress, and this notion of progress can apparently substitute for the ends pursued. As long as we change, there is progress, and as a result we are approaching this very vague and hypothetical goal that the nineteenth century exploited with delirium and romanticism.

We no longer wonder in the least what these ends consist in or see clearly the direction in which we are headed. Control is no longer possible, because ends have disappeared or seem disconnected from the means that

---

2. Lenin, *State and Revolution*, 80–81.

3. Ellul's book on art is *The Empire of Non-Sense*. (DG)

4. That is, Nazi.

occupy the entire scope of people's activity, attention, and admiration. We do still talk about happiness, freedom, or justice, but we no longer know their content or conditions, and we come out with these empty phrases only to take steps that bear no relation to these illusions. Once these ends have become implicit in people's hearts and minds, they no longer have any formative power. They no longer have creative capacity. They are dead illusions that have been stored away among the props of the contemporary scene. They can no longer be taken seriously. No one is willing to die for them; instead, they will die for their "bread and butter"[5] or because they have become means themselves—the means of a party, nation, or class. And as means, they are thrown into a battle that is directed toward no end. The heroism of a soldier in war or of a laborer on strike is in reality the heroism of a means that does not actually know where it is going.

These impotent ends are completely incapable of creating means that accord with the end. The end can now no longer inspire, because it is nothing more than a word. It is not even a myth! It no longer creates anything. The way that means are created is entirely different: they are mutually self-generating.

Just as genius is no longer necessary for the majority of technical discoveries, but having arrived at a certain stage the next discovery comes along almost as a matter of course, so also genius is no longer necessary in politics. Circumstances and technical means dictate to politicians what they must do. So also, in every field, means drive the creation of new means. In the order of industrial, financial, political, and other means, a strict law of mechanical causality obtains. Human beings barely intervene. New sectors of production appear, because new machines have been created or new means found to exploit raw material that was previously unknown. It doesn't matter that people do not need these new products, or that these new creations are completely useless. One means generates another. A particular one is used, for why would it not be? Why would it be called useless? An end would be needed by which it could be measured, but there are no more ends. And this self-production of means entails a very remarkable result: the definitive confirmation that ends are absent.[6]

---

5. The French idiom is *bifteck* (beefsteak), referring to one's livelihood or basic rights.

6. "Technique is nothing more than means and the ensemble of means. . . . Our civilization is first and foremost a civilization of means; in the reality of modern life, the means, it would seem, are more important than the ends." *The Technological Society*, 19. (DG)

We have seen how the sought-for goal has become implicit, abstract. This accomplished, it has remained inert. We still have the same notions of happiness or freedom as a century ago, degraded and weakened. Yet the development of means makes these ends absurd! The means have shattered the very possibility of relying on traditional ends, but we have not even conceived that the means that are in play lead to the negation of implicit ends. We congratulate ourselves each time an airplane surpasses a speed record, and we make great efforts to succeed in going faster, as if speed were a good and sufficient goal in itself. But what is the point of saving time?

We rejoice each time that a new cure is found; much research is carried out in order that we might heal better. But what is the point of the life that we take so much care to preserve? What is time for? What is life worth, when precisely through the interplay of the means set in motion in this civilization, time and life no longer have any meaning, when human beings really do not know what to do with their time, and when life is more absurd than ever, because the spiritual foundations of time and life have been destroyed in their hearts? Modern people—dehumanized through means, having become means—are, when they are given time and their life is preserved for them, like people living a traditional way of life who are given a complex machine but don't know how to use it.[7]

But even more, see how we are stripped of both our time and our life that we have taken so much trouble to obtain. For no civilization has been as wasteful of the time and lives of human beings. Immense forces will be put into service so that one person can save a few seconds, while full days will be lost to the unemployed and to those waiting in queues at government offices. Both are products of the enormity of our means.[8]

All possible knowledge will be put into play to save one life, but millions of people will be massacred through bombs and concentration camps; both are products of the enormity of our means. For everything around us, the same parallel can be made. Security? We very ably work out a prodigious governmental machine[9] in order to assure social security to people. But why? For what purpose? Because, after all, no time has been as uncertain as our own. And what is this pitiful security being offered to human

---

7. Literally, *like savages who are given a complex machine and whose hands lack the skill to use it.*

8. The irony is that technique, while resolutely following the rule of efficiency and the "one best way," so often leads to bureaucratic delay and inefficiency. It clashes with human reality and cannot fully subjugate us. (DG)

9. *Machine administrative*, referring to the provision of government services.

beings, a few million francs, at the cost of the insecurity that comes from financial, social, and economic crises, wars and revolutions, which, thanks to our technical means, now endanger all men, women, and children? In this frightful round of unchecked means, nobody knows any longer where they are going, purposes are forgotten, and ends are overtaken. Human beings have set off at astronomically high speeds toward nowhere.

* * *

The second characteristic of this question as it is presented today is that the means is self-justifying. We have left behind the principle that "the end justifies the means." Of course, there are still theoreticians who uphold this idea and construct systems on this basis, such as communists, and some moralistic people are still naive enough to be scandalized by the idea and situate the problem at the moral level. But in reality, all this comes from the way of thinking that accords with a time when human beings had spiritual and intellectual mastery over their means, when they could choose among several kinds of means and would choose the one that seemed most apt for attaining the desired end. If this means was morally reprehensible, it was accepted because of the end's loftiness and beauty. But this era has been over now for almost a century, and it is quite comical to see politicians, who claim to be modern and free of prejudice, adopting this rule as a principle of action. The facts themselves have made the system outdated, the principle inapplicable, and the ideas obsolete.

In reality, what justifies the means today is whatever succeeds. Whatever is effective, whatever possesses in itself an "efficiency,"[10] is justified. By applying means, a result is produced. This result is judged by these simplistic criteria of "more": larger, faster, more precise, and so on. Simply by applying this criterion, the means is declared good. What succeeds is good, what fails is bad. Now, technique teaches us how to infallibly discern the means, the one means that carries within it the success that is most spectacular. Technique always succeeds. The most-perfected technical means attains necessarily all technical objectives (which are not ends—confusion must be carefully avoided). A politics of means will be therefore a triumphant politics. The communist economy, which is an economy entirely focused on means, therefore produces incomparable successes, and as long as it stays focused in this way it will advance quickly (although human beings

10. Ellul uses the English word *efficiency*.

may of course starve to death during this time!). The German army, a triumph of technical means, represents therefore a kind of success, because an enemy that was four times larger took four years to destroy it. Examples of this sort are easy to find.

The triumph of this approach is easy to explain. Once the means becomes a matter of technique it knows no bounds. It applies itself indifferently to all objects and recognizes no rule except technical laws. It has no concern with value judgment. It can be nothing but an instrument that functions well. And it is true that value judgments (good or bad, just or unjust) normally concern the end and not the means. As a result, the technical process finds itself free of all ideological or moral obstacle. It functions entirely like a machine, without any external value to trouble its well-functioning cogs and pistons. It is sometimes the case that the technical results, such as concentration camps, make ordinary people recoil in horror, but this is simply because they have been outside the technical means' operations. A Russian communist does not recoil from camps in Siberia, or a Nazi from extermination camps. When the practice has spread throughout the world, when we are all within the mechanism of this "means," no one will be appalled any longer.

This process of "self-justification"[11] has three outcomes. The first is that human beings are no longer to any extent the masters of their means. This is an observation that is often made, and the sorcerer's apprentice[12] does not date from today. It is useless to insist, but an often neglected aspect of this idea is that human beings no longer have the choice of means. They no longer have at their disposal an arsenal of processes to attain a result, among which their personality can exercise a choice. Technique chooses for them. And it chooses with a precision and cleverness that human beings cannot match. It shows them the one means that is truly effective, and after all, why would people refuse it? Thus the responsibility for making use of one means is radically cut off; there is no choice. It will likely be said that this isn't the case everywhere: [it does not apply, for example, to] medicine, politics, law, or economics. But these techniques are still in their infancy, and human beings still choose because technique's advance in these fields is slow. But this infant is growing up quickly, and we are already familiar

---

11. Ellul uses the English word *self-justification*.

12. A junior magician who has enough knowledge to unleash a power but not enough to then control it. The most well-known version of this story is "Der Zauberlehrling" ("The Sorcerer's Apprentice"), a poem by Johann Wolfgang von Goethe (1749–1832).

with its adult face. In a century, in these fields, human beings will have the best means possible, unarguably. They will be the same everywhere over the entire earth, and they will live in peace—*Resquiescat in pace.*[13]

A second result is that technique is extended into all areas. To the very extent that ends disappear and human beings no longer have the choice of means, but one solitary path opens to their desires for action, they extend technique over all objects. This fact, which we will take up again, occurs all the more easily because technique is declared neutral. We have retained the classic belief, soothing in this agitated world, refreshing in our hell, that means are insignificant, that they are secondary in relation to the ends that are so noble and right that we must pursue. They are negligible and neutral. A table is neutral, from the point of view of good and evil; a machine must be neutral, too. By extension, so is the organization of labor, as well as government or psychotechnique, or the technique of propaganda—but then so too the missile or the concentration camp! In reality, when we say that technique seems neutral what we mean is that deep within ourselves we all think it is good. Technique is good because it extends the power of human beings, and means are justified today by the power that they give to human beings. This is the meaning of this self-justification that I was speaking about earlier. But this is in fact a theological discussion and does not belong here. We are concerned only with noting this firm conviction of human beings that intensifies the phenomenon of means.

Finally, a third result is that all the ends that human beings propose for these exclusive means that technique places at their disposal are clearly useless or inadequate. The means no longer needs an end, since it is justified in advance. Here we find all the ridiculousness and tragedy of those who want to offer new ends to our technical civilization. By the very fact that it is technical, there are no longer any goals that can possibly be assigned. It goes forward where each step takes it, the blind leading the blind,[14] a relentless monster that nothing can repel. Idealists of Huxley's type claim to subordinate our means to a new end, choosing the best means because bad means vitiate ends. These intentions are honorable and objectively correct, but they are as out of place in our day as is opposing a tank by throwing rocks. The same goes for the church that seeks ends to propose to technical human beings: they are necessarily ineffective. Technical human beings do not need goals in life; they are content with the instant success of means.

13. Latin for *May he/she rest in peace,* a phrase used in relation to the dead.
14. Matt 15:14; Luke 6:39.

In fact, we have got hold here of the primary reason, which is decisive and unique in its depth, that the church and Christianity have lost ground. If the church no longer seems relevant in the world, it is because of the new situation of the problem of means.

This fact that technique is self-justifying has a theological root that is worth pointing out in passing. It is obvious. Genesis 3:6: "The woman saw that the tree was good for food, that it was pleasant to the sight, and that it was desirable for opening the mind . . . ." Satan uses the obvious fact as a means of persuading human beings to act, without having convinced them. One does not argue with obvious facts. One does not argue with penicillin or with an airplane that goes more than 1,000 km an hour. And we have such need of this deadly, obvious fact to give us confidence! But again, we are not seeking to do theology here, but to study facts.

* * *

The third characteristic of the problem of means today is that they are totalitarian. Our civilization is entirely one of means, and means affect every domain. They respect nothing. This totalitarian reality can be considered from two angles. We have already indicated one of them briefly.

First, means have become exclusive of all that does not aid their progress or is not compatible with their forward motion. On the one hand, the means will destroy everything that might restrict its development. Thus technique will attack and then destroy, in turn, moral judgment (and therefore morality as a whole), humanism, which claims to subordinate everything to human beings (but technique does not accept being limited by the interest of human beings), and gratuitousness, because everything must serve (thus art for art's sake must be replaced by art for the community or the regime), as well as awareness (because it is essential that human beings be blind, so that they can be good slaves of the means that are developed). Technique will abolish the critical faculty in order to develop itself at last in freedom—for the greatest good of "humanity," of course. In the same way, people used to put out the eyes of nightingales so that they would sing more beautifully. And the means, triumphant upon the ruins of human values, constructs its own values that will aid its ascent. All new "values" are props for means, such as the new myths. State, nation, race, proletariat, labor, all that political parties offer us as spiritual values, are in fact only the artificial scenery in which technique advances. They are the illusion offered to human beings to make them accept this desert, the appearance that hides the appalling desiccation of the world they are living in.

But actually these new myths have an effect that is not adequately stressed: they place the spiritual in the service of means. They enable the use of what appeared until then useless in human beings (and which Marxist realism rejected for this reason). This is the great discovery of the USA, which uses Christianity just like a factor of labor, then of fascist dictatorships that use spiritual forces for the material power of the nation, and finally communism seems to have caught on to the idea and begun in its turn to use myths of whatever kind, even Christian ones, for the dictatorship of the proletariat. This subordination of the spiritual to technical means is the great revolution, in fact the only one, that our age has been able to produce—which means that it is the full stop placed before all [real] revolutionary possibility.

The second aspect of this totalitarianism of means is that they succeed little by little in extending their dominion over everything. Not only are material objects submitted to technique, but also human beings. Human beings are no longer subjects; they become in their turn objects of the powers that they have created. Self-knowledge no longer leads to self-mastery; now self-knowledge leads to the enslavement of self. The means no longer discloses one's true image; it now reduces one to the condition of "facsimile." And the psychotechnique is worked out more thoroughly, along with labor camps, propaganda, and managed leisure, just as human breeding programs and human vivisection will become common in a few years' time. We have explained elsewhere what the logical steps have been, and the necessity. And the autocracy of means overcomes the spiritual domain: spiritual problems have today become problems of means to use. It is enough to refer to a certain American conception of spiritual questions, studied for example in *Elmer Gantry* (by S. Lewis).[15] But this leads inevitably to emptying these spiritual means of all substance. Because human beings have become objects and the spiritual is classed among spiritual means, existence no longer has any possible meaning. Existentialism, the philosophy of our time, is correct to remind us that our existence is such, but it is incorrect in saying that human beings are free to restore meaning

---

15. *Elmer Gantry*, a novel by Sinclair Lewis (1885–1951) that satirizes white fundamentalist American religion.

to their lives. The irreversible triumph of means eliminates any freedom for human beings to follow this path. To still believe that human beings have this angel-like power is to understand neither our times nor ourselves.

2

We are caught in a trap. It is useless to act smart and claim to have inner freedom. When a freedom is not part of my life, it is false. For Christians, this situation is particularly dreadful, because what we have described is precisely the proof that living out our faith, bearing an authentic witness, is today impossible. We know of course that living out one's faith has always been impossible, and we find it easy to console ourselves by saying that our day is no worse than the others and the difficulties are the same. But this is not true! That it has always been impossible to live out one's faith, yes, [that is true, but] for internal reasons.[16] "Wretched man that I am, to do the evil that I will not and not do the good that I would!"[17] But today it is for external reasons, too. In no civilization until our own have human beings ever been so totally constrained. They may have been the slaves of hunger, natural circumstances, or other people, yet they always preserved a margin of freedom sufficient to remain masters of the majority of their time and to choose among various options. (Only history books, stupidly imbued with the glory of the nineteenth century, have claimed otherwise, but it has become a current idea!) All civilizations have exercised certain constraints, but they left to each person a wide field of freedom and individuality. The Roman slave or the medieval serf was more free, more individual, more socially human (I do not say more materially content) than is the modern worker or Soviet functionary. Our civilization, which claims that it does not exercise any constraints, tries to seize human beings in their totality and confine them within a detailed framework, in which all their gestures and secret thoughts will be controlled by the social system.

This is what the triumph of means represents. This is the new fact that obstructs the living out of the Christian faith. So Christians must

---

16. Ellul argues again in extreme dialectical fashion: the Christian life is *impossible* not just because of our broken and corrupted interior soul and spirit, but because the surrounding culture of technique eliminates our freedom and makes all of our choices for us. *Impossible*—but still *necessary* to resist and to act—and so in the end *possible*. (DG)

17. Rom 7:15–24.

understand in a precise way that their testimony and action have become impossible because of these circumstances also [in addition to the internal constraints that have always been present]. They must understand that if they do not break this supremacy of means, this will be (excepting a miracle) the end of Christianity's social expression and soon thereafter of its individual one, because faith in Jesus Christ will not long survive in this rarefied atmosphere. This dictatorship must be broken. Christians must engage in a struggle "not against flesh and blood, but against powers, thrones, dominations!"[18] And they must understand that this struggle, which is first principally spiritual, is a fight to the death. Rimbaud's saying is truer than ever here: "Spiritual combat is as brutal as men's battle!"[19]

I will not speak here of what ought to be, a subject that is too platonic for a discussion as urgent as this. Neither will I suggest means of action, [which would result only in] opposing one technique to others. I will simply remind us of a path that is an old Christian road, abandoned for some two hundred years, and which leads in the opposite direction from the triumphal path of modern techniques.

* * *

The first truth that must be recalled is that for Christians there is no separation between end and means. It is a Greek and moralizing way of thinking that has produced this separation. Our starting point is that in the work of God, end and means are brought together. Thus when Jesus Christ is present, the kingdom has come. This statement makes the relationship between end and means very clear. Jesus Christ, in his incarnation, appears as God's means for the salvation of human beings and for the establishing of God's kingdom. But there where Jesus Christ is, there also is this salvation and kingdom.

This is the very opposite of our situation today as we have described it. Whereas our civilization absorbs end into means, in God's action the means never appears except as the realized presence of the end. The end, this kingdom, that will come at the end of time, is already here today, when the means of God (the mediator, the one and only!) is present! All of God's action is precisely to bring into being, through his means, the end that is his work. And whether [we consider] the covenant, law, prophets, history, or

18. Eph 6:12.

19. From the poem "Une Saison en Enfer" by Arthur Rimbaud (1854–91).

wisdom of Israel,[20] it is always the same act of God manifesting this unity of end and means. It must be so therefore in the entire Christian life. For Christians also, end and means are united in this same way. They can only oppose with all their might, then, our slavery to means. But especially, they must take on a different stance. They should not first draw up plans, programs, and means of action and results. When Christians do these things (and it is an epidemic today in the church), it is a simple imitation of the world, which is bound to fail. What we are able to do has no importance whatsoever if we do not bear "engagement with a good conscience toward God."[21]

What counts are not our instruments and institutions, but ourselves, because it is we ourselves who are God's instruments. And because the church and all its members are God's means, they must be this presence of the end that characterizes the kingdom. So we need never seek an objective external to ourselves, which would have to be attained at the cost of great effort (all efforts are accomplished in Jesus Christ!). Instead, we must bear within ourselves the objective toward which God is orienting the world. Regardless of whether we like it or whether others call it pride, Christians are not in the same situation as others concerning this end: they have received this end within themselves through God's grace. They must represent before the world this unity of end and means, of which Jesus Christ is the guarantor. For human beings are not the ones who establish this end as such or who bring it into being. It is God who determines and realizes it.

This [way of understanding our situation] completely reverses the attitude that is current among people who do their work and then add, as a supererogatory precaution, that "Of course, it is God who gives the increase,"[22] or again, "Do what I must, let come what may," or again, "Man proposes, but God disposes," and so on. All this [is only the] wisdom of the nations, human wisdom that seeks to enlist God on its side. In this whole attitude, there is actually a separation between the work of human beings and of God, between means and end. It is an understanding of life that is radically anti-Christian, to the extent that people are invited to attend to their own business and God is added in from some sense of decorum derived from a bygone age! Quite to the contrary, we see that God establishes his end and it is this end that is represented through our means. The

---

20. That is, whether we consider any part of the Old Testament.

21. 1 Pet 3:21.

22. 1 Cor 3:6.

direction is reversed. And this has an extraordinarily practical significance; it is not an intellectual game.[23]

It means, for example, that we do not have to labor and strive for justice to reign on the earth; we ourselves must be just, bearers of justice.[24] Scripture teaches us that justice reigns where the just person is. Of course, *just* means justified by Christ, and it is for this very reason that justice reigns where a just person is, because the just live by the justice of Christ. This justice is present because it is what makes them just. So it does not appear as a goal to attain or a balance to reach but as the gift of God, free and inexplicable, existing in our life, so that our means do not bring justice about but show it forth. In the same way, there is no need for us to try, through great labor and skill, to bring peace on earth. Instead, we ourselves must be peaceful. For where the peaceful are, there peace reigns.

This same idea prevails [in all areas of life]. This creation by God of good goals, such as peace, this living creation in Jesus Christ, can only be *expressed*, nothing more, through our means. The principle of a Christian ethic therefore flows from this: we must seek in Scripture what must be lived out, so that the end that God desires may become present in people's midst. All ethics has for object not the attainment of a goal (and we are quite aware that for an authentically Christian morality, sanctity must not be *sought*!) but the manifestation of the gift that is given to us, of grace and peace, love and expression of the Holy Spirit, which is to say, exactly the end that God seeks and that is miraculously present within us. From this point forward, our human understanding of means is turned radically upside down. It is cut free from its root in pride and power. The means is no longer called upon to "accomplish" anything whatever. It is delivered from its uncertainty about the path to follow and the success to hope for. We can liquidate at good price the obsession with means by which our time is gripped. And in the church, we must learn that it is not our possibilities that direct our action, but it is indeed God's end, present within us!

I am quite familiar with the reproach that will likely be made. This is an individual pursuit, it will be said once again, an individualistic notion of action, when the great discovery of our time ([admittedly][25] great and

23. See Ellul's *The Meaning of the City*, especially chapter 5, section 3: "From Eden to Jerusalem," 173–82 for a description of how God adopts and redeems the city. (DG)

24. The French noun *justice* may be translated as *justice* or *righteousness*, and the French adjective *juste* as *just*, *justified*, or *righteous*.

25. The meaning is unclear, but presumably Ellul is indicating that he does not deny the value of collective action.

good) is that action must be collective. It is to return to the individual level problems that go beyond one individual and concern everyone. It means once again finding an individual solution to questions that are not individual and that do not concern us only but are also problems of institutions. Peace and justice are in this way matters of political and social organization, and as a result we must have adequate means, we must locate the problem elsewhere than in the individual consciousness.[26]

These arguments are invalid, in fact. It is not a matter here of opposing an individualistic notion of action to a collective one, or an institutional one. Concerning the first objection, it is enough to point out that it is not a question of the individual, but of God. It is not a matter of *our* peace or *our* justice, but those that God gives. As a result, this whole notion of means is not centered on the individual, but on God, and by this very fact it is a collective notion, because it is God who produces this action's unity and it is God who acts in us, "who works in us to will and to do."[27] As it is one God acting in all through one Spirit, the collective unity of these means is assured, not through our human means but through the very unity of God.

Of course, this is an idea of community and unity that exposes our unbelief.[28] To the extent that we refuse to put our confidence in God and want to ensure our action, make it rational, take charge of it, and give it the form we want, we refuse to let go of the anthropocentric dilemma: individual or community. For the way out is precisely the action of God, which opens up the way for us. God's action is concerned with the human person, always a relationship between a person and God, but it is also collective through God, because God is the same for all. In this way, this idea of means evades traditional categories.

On the second point, the stance with regard to institutions, it must be said that the pursuit of means acting indirectly on individual persons, the quest to modify institutions in order ultimately to change the human condition, is hypocrisy or a lie. When we are scandalized because institutional modification (property, distribution, government, and so on) is not the main concern, it can signify only two things. Either we are conscious Marxists, and we do not believe in the existence of a human nature but only of a human condition, which can be totally and radically modified by

---

26. The French noun *conscience* may be translated as *conscience* or *consciousness*.

27. Phil 2:13.

28. *Qui déçoit notre incrédulité*, that disappoints our incredulity. The meaning is unclear.

54

institutional change (but this is then the opposite of creation), or else we are hypocrites, and we refuse to pose the problem of the human in its fullness, we refuse to look at it straight on and consider only its environment. We turn our eyes from the being's picture in order to look only at the frame. If it is true that the frame can more or less enhance the picture, it is not true that it is what gives the picture its value.[29] And if we act in this way, it means that we refuse to be fully involved to this venture.

All this does not mean that changing institutions has no importance. But such change is not what has priority. In any case, the mad pursuit for means to change these institutions, a pursuit that we witness today, is an error before God and utterly pointless. (There is no need to be a Christian to perceive this.) As a result, it is perfectly valid to pursue institutional reforms, as long as this pursuit comes out of our fundamental position, which is to say, a pure and simple expression of the presence of the end in the world, and the transformation is carried out through the living presence, in the contemporary world, of the end and of judgment.

A very simple example can be taken from one of the social reforms that came out of Christianity. Slavery was gradually suppressed during the third and fourth centuries not through decrees or a direct condemnation of slavery by the church and Christians, but because the Christians of the time felt a profound equality with their slaves because of their continual expectation of Christ's return. It became useless and unjust to have slaves, because Christ was coming soon! Institutional reforms must come out of the church's faith and not from the technical competence of specialists, whether Christian or otherwise.

* * *

But if it is indeed true that this end should hold such a place in the world and be the only point of reference possible for our epoch, this leads to an unprecedented upheaval among the enormous means that our civilization has delighted in accumulating. We must see here what this actually signifies.

The first observation to strike us is that our means are completely unsuited to the single end that has worth. As a result, when we observe that our means have no goal, this is indeed the truth. There is an immense gap between these means and the sole end; and by this fact they are radically

29. A play on words: *Et s'il est vrai que le cadre peut mettre plus ou moins en valeur* (enhance) *l'image, il n'est pas vrai que ce soit lui qui lui donne sa valeur* (value).

ineffective. "But," one will say (and I am thinking of the technicians,[30] scandalized by such "confusion"!), "you are confusing what should remain separate. We have never claimed to bring about the kingdom of God through our technique. Our means are adapted to immediate goals. You do not have the right to condemn them in the name of Christ's return. These are two different orders. There are spiritual values, with Christ's return at the end, and there are material values. Or again, there is the order of grace and the order of preservation. There is grace and there is law," and so on, and so on.

We reject this argument completely. First, because in fact technicians have indeed claimed to be bringing about the kingdom of God on earth: this is precisely what the notion of Progress means, brilliantly illustrated by Victor Hugo, Renan, and several others![31] It is also precisely what the theological doctrine corresponds to that rejects the catastrophic coming of the kingdom and believes in its gradual appearance, the ascension of humanity toward God. That is where the confusion occurs, and not with us!

Next, because it is false to separate two orders, matter and spirit, grace and law, and so on. In reality, the two orders, of preservation and redemption, are not separate but integrated with each other. All the actions of human beings are in submission to the Lordship of Jesus Christ. The means are indeed ordered to this one end. But when we say that they are ineffective, this does not mean that they cannot bring about the kingdom of God. It means that *human beings' means* (technical or other) *are ineffective for accomplishing their particular ends, because human beings have rejected the reality of the one, absolute end.* Thus econometrics will totally fail to regulate economic life, because it assumes that the economy functions in isolation rather than in submission to the present judgment of Christ's return. This may seem improbable, but it is the fruit of revelation. All technique becomes dead when it is not ordered, situated, and judged by the kingdom of God that is coming.

And this is the second conclusion that we can draw: all the means at our disposal, all these technical means that the modern world has created in its pride and intoxication—money, mechanical power, propaganda, the cinema, the press, modern conveniences, or means of communication, all this pandemonium of noise in which bewildered human beings do not know how to find their way—can be restored to their place if they are

---

30. That is, people who are technically oriented or minded.

31. Victor Hugo (1802–85), poet and novelist. Ernst Renan (1823–92), philosopher and historian.

situated from the perspective of this end that is already present in the means that God uses. It is certainly not a case here of abolishing or casting aside these means of civilization, not an arbitrary transcendentalism founded on the power of the human spirit,[32] not an optimism concerning this venture's outcome, for we are not at all saying that it must happen. We are simply stating the singular and essential condition by which these means may finally be directed to making the lives of human beings possible.

The foregoing assumes an attitude that is resolutely hostile to political realism. It is an attitude that places means under judgment, not in the name of moral rules but in virtue of this existing presence of the end that God desires. In order for these means to be truly ordered in relation to this eschatological coming, they must cease to be unlimited and devoid of criteria that transcend themselves. They are judged; they are accepted or rejected. It is not their intrinsic virtue, their technical efficacy, or their quality as means that counts; it is their eschatological content, their ability to be integrated into the Lordship of Jesus Christ. They are not good or bad; they are called to enter into the kingdom of love, and they may or may not enter it. They are within or without the gates of the heavenly Jerusalem. Their glory may or may not be brought as an offering to God's glory. It is therefore not some external and superadded quality of these means that is under consideration; it is their situation itself. Nor is it their immediate purpose or result, but their very content. And this is to say, then, that they should be viewed less as means of something than as activities of human beings.

This is the most significant step to take. We have seen how God's work invited us to do away with the distinction between end and means, and how our action is no longer a means but, to the very extent that it expresses an act of God, a presence of the end. And now we are brought to the point of denying that any purely human activity is a means, all this human labor that today occupies our field of vision.

In reality it is no longer a means of anything. It is only an activity, nothing else, and as activity it is also subordinate to this conception of means that the Christian faith shows us. But this activity is not wild and incoherent, as might be supposed. It is instead perfectly oriented and ordered. It is shaped by all of these pursuits of modern human beings, but put in their place and deprived of their colossal tragedy. It is no longer true, in this fundamental unity of end and means, in this authentic operation of means, that all this production of modern civilization is the necessary

32. The French noun *esprit* may be translated as *spirit* or *mind*.

condition for happiness, the cause of progress, and so forth. It is no longer through the increase of means that we may hope to finally discover a value and a virtue; it is no longer on mechanical power that the future of humanity will depend. Instead of a march from past to future, an incoming tide of the future explains and informs the present, in such a way that our technical discoveries are never anything but temporary moves, to be assigned their exact place according to the perspective of the kingdom. But this act of placement assumes that secondary ends can be assigned, restricted to these instruments. They are useful for something.

Thanks to this new relation between end and means, we can say exactly what they are called to serve and what we can expect from them. We have here, then, something quite different from ends absorbed into means or from philosophical ends that have no connection with means. In a certain sense, we have a way of applying a common measure to all these powers, through their relation to the already present Lordship of Christ. We can now seek in Scripture reforms to carry out and God's temporary order for the world, as long as we understand their relative value and that the means used to bring about these results are not ultimately ordered to them or judged by them. Instead, they are ordered to the kingdom of God and judged by it. In this way, we find our activities' true value and their true relation with the secondary ends that we may propose.

* * *

Yet this attempt to restore means to their true situation, to give back to human activity its orientation, is only one more ideology that is ineffective and worthless if it is not accompanied by a deeper transformation. We see concretely that the world is lost if it does not recover, through a spiritual revolution, a transcendent end that is nonetheless immanent, already present, an end the presence of which should be perceptible also in the rarefied world of techniques. Now, we can search through all the philosophies; Christianity alone offers an answer. But again, that is easy to say and quickly settled; that doesn't change anything. Christians must understand their responsibility in this venture, because Christianity (and God) will not act necessarily in this way. This venture is not the history that unfolds whether we wish it or not. It may become actual, or it may not. God may act, and he may not, and when God wants to act he needs to find instruments receptive to his action. Let us constantly recall the lesson given in

Scripture that God rarely acts in a direct and transcendent fashion. Instead, he always chooses for himself a human instrument to carry out his work. In this work of God, decisive in the actual[33] (and also in the purely spiritual sphere, since there is still the question of knowing whether we will remain in this present dilemma: Jesus Christ expelled from the world by means, or Jesus Christ integrated in the world and himself become a means!), will God find the necessary partners? In other words, does this recognition, that God's revelation in Jesus Christ is what alone provides a valid response to the current impossible problem of end and means, entail consequences in the lives of those who today call themselves Christians? Is it something other than a mere intellectual position?

In fact, here is where the preceding chapter joins up with this one. Our attitude in the face of end and means requires us to take up a stance that is completely revolutionary. It means a radical change in the view of human life. The conclusion that Christians must put into practice is that at the present time it is a matter of "being" and not "doing."

Our world is completely oriented toward action. Everything is expressed in terms of actions, nothing is finer than action, and we seek slogans, programs, means of action. Our world is in the process of losing its life because of action. We know that the great slogan of all dictatorships is "Action for the sake of action." In this way, we return to this problem of end and means.

But at the same time, our world tends to destroy individual life almost entirely. By the formation of masses, the artificial creation of myths, the standardization of lifestyles, and so forth, a general movement toward uniformity occurs, and individual persons are drawn more and more into self-forgetfulness in the flood tide of this general manifold that is mechanical civilization. People who spend their time in action cease in this way even to live. People at the steering wheel of their cars, which run for hours at 120 km an hour, have the sensation of living through speed, acting, and "gaining" time. But a mental stupor overtakes them, and they become increasingly stupid, a machine operating a machine. They have reflexes and sensations but no judgment or awareness. They have lost their souls in the perfect whir of their engine. Thus are we all, in our general torpor that may end in agony.

But if what we have said about Christianity is true—the necessity for Christians to represent the end in present events, restore a perspective

33. That is, in physical reality.

to the world, rediscover the secondary ends for activity itself—then this implies that action is no longer sovereign, and that the necessary attitude is to live, refusing the action that the world proposes to us.

The central problem that arises for Christians *today* is not of knowing how to act, or of choosing from the innumerable forms of action that the world proposes to us, or of acting for or against or otherwise. When we see the countless efforts toward action that the churches make, when we hear the speeches and the calls to action ("Let us march, march"[34]) and the platforms, when we see, for example, that in the political sphere Christians do not want to get beyond this ridiculous question, "Should we act for or against communism?" when we see that all that is written above will inevitably raise questions that I am very familiar with: "So you are against the machine? or techniques?" etc. and, "How can we act in these circumstances to change . . . ," when we see all this—we cannot avoid being gripped by fear before this wretched imitation of the world, the works of the prince of this world!

Christians are so imbued with the fundamental doctrines of the world that they no longer have any freedom of thought or life, and yet "you were bought at a price; do not become slaves of human beings!" (1 Cor 7:23). Today, *this* is what is happening: to be slaves of human beings means adopting the world's basic premises, having its prejudices and reactions. We have lost the meaning of true action that is the evidence of a deep life, action that comes from the heart, that is the product of faith and not of myth, propaganda, and Mammon! It is a matter of living, not of doing, and that is the revolutionary attitude in this world, which wants only (useful) action and not life at all. We must take seriously the spiritual powers that are enclosed within the fact of being spiritually alive. We must cease believing that life depends on vitamins, hormones, and physical exercise. We must get rid of the *mens sana in corpore sano*,[35] which is exactly the right way to get rid of life for the sake of action.

That people might be alive instead of obsessed with doing—this is the reality that may enable means to be restored to their rightful place. But it clearly means a radical break with *all* trends of the present day. But again, to be alive, what does that mean? It partly involves the intellectual life, the characteristics of which we will examine in the next chapter. But it is above

---

34. Perhaps a reference to the refrain of "La Marseillaise," the French national song.

35. Latin for *a sound mind in a sound body*, a pagan (classical) slogan to express well-being.

all a fact of spiritual life. To be alive is the complete situation of human beings placed before God, and this is precisely what our world wants to obviate and make us forget, through its philosophies and thought: materialism, spiritualism, surrealism, existentialism, and essentialism, or through its concrete action, about which we have said enough. In all areas, an immense effort is made to keep people from being in this complete situation where they are alive.

These are the truths of doctrine, the living depths of which we can never fathom: creature and image of God, creatures that are judged, condemned in justice, forgiven and saved in love; unique, irreplaceable creatures (who have become unique because the Son of God died for each one, called to Christian freedom through sanctification and regaining a free life to the glory of the Creator), called to the renewal of their mind and to bear in themselves the truth of God: "Do you not know that your bodies are the temple of the Holy Spirit?" (1 Cor 6:19), called to judge all things, because "You will judge even the angels" (1 Cor 6:3) and to participate in the glorious coming of the Lord of lords; all this through the Holy Spirit's life in us: "You have been called from death to life."[36] And there is no other life; but we still need to live it out and not let it wither away under the influence of the spirits of the world.

What constrains us is that we no longer conceive of action except in the rational form of mechanical means. We no longer conceive of it in the form that we are constantly reminded of in Scripture: the grain that works, the leaven that causes the dough to rise, the light that drives out the darkness, and so on.[37] Yet this is the action required of us, because this is how the Holy Spirit works. So it is the fact of living, with all its consequences, all its twists and turns, that is the revolutionary act *par excellence* and also the answer to this problem of end and means. In a civilization that no longer knows what life is, the most useful thing that Christians can do is precisely to live, and the life held in faith has a remarkably explosive power. We no longer realize it, because we no longer believe in anything but efficiency, and life is not efficient. But it—it alone—can provoke the astonishment of the modern world by revealing to everyone the ineffectiveness of techniques.

Once again, in closing, we will specify that when we speak of life we are not referring to a mysticism of the inner life or a biological or hermetic vitalism of any sort. We are referring to the expression of the Holy Spirit

36. Rom 6:13.

37. Matt 5:14; 13:31–33; Luke 13:19–21.

working within us and being expressed in our material life through our words, habits, and decisions. We are speaking, then, of rediscovering all that the fullness of personal life signifies for human beings, standing on their own feet, within the world, and who can recognize their neighbors again, because they themselves have been recognized by God. In the powerful presence of the Holy Spirit, we receive the response to this work of God. And we feel deflated, because we are no longer very sure of the course ahead, and it no longer depends on us. End as well as means are taken from us, we hesitate on this open road with its unknown outcome, and we now have only one certainty, the promise that we are given of a certain order whose guarantor is God: "Seek first the kingdom of God and his righteousness, and all the rest will be given to you" (Matt 6:33).

All that we have said about end and means, the eschatological nature of the unity between end and means, the fact that the result does not depend on us, the necessity of living and not doing—all this is only the interpretation and the message for today of these words of Jesus.

And we ourselves can no longer live today except by the promise that, truly, *all the rest* will be given us in addition to the kingdom, which is, for us, both promised and granted.

CHAPTER FOUR

Communication

This title may appear puzzling to those who are not used to intellectual vocabulary. Actually the question being raised here is very basic: it concerns the situation and work of Christian intellectuals.[1] But again, it will be asked, what does this have to do with being present in the world? Aren't intellectuals just members of the church as others are, neither greater nor less? Do they still think they are somehow superior, after the world's wisdom has been so harshly condemned (1 Cor 1–2)? And besides, aren't we already overburdened by the writings of intellectuals, particularly this new theology that is so intellectual![2]

It is certainly true that Christian intellectuals are laypeople in the church like others. But it is also true that as intellectuals they necessarily have a particular function, in the world and in the church. They cannot avoid doing theology, because their vocation as intellectuals calls them to think out their faith. But they need not be specialists in theology; they are laypeople. They do not need to undertake any kind of academic theology.[3]

1. Ellul is referring in this context to educated men and women who by choice, practice, and often by vocation, read, think, discuss, write, and teach about truth and reality from a Christian point of view. Not only professional theologians and pastors but also some members of the laity play this role. Terms such as *thoughtful Christians* and *Christian leaders* might be good substitutes for Ellul's references to *Christian intellectuals*. (DG)

2. Ellul may be referring to twentieth-century theological giants such as Karl Barth (1886–1968). (DG)

3. *Théologie speculative*, theology that is oriented to theoretical questions rather

Given their involvement in the world and its activities, however, they do need to undertake a kind of practical theology. They must very carefully think out their situation as Christians involved in the world—and think out their faith in their relations with the world. So they have a very specific function [in the church] that no one else can do in their stead. Given the decadence of the civilization we live in, though, Christian intellectuals also have a very specific mission toward the world, which we need to define here. Our task in fact is to consider presence in the world, rather than the role within the church. We will leave aside the problems of Christian culture and what we might call "professional theology"!

Yet in the objection to intellectuals that I raised above, there is still a point that needs emphasizing. It is true that intellectuals are no greater in the church than others, and it is wrong to set forth an over-intellectualized theology (but is it not also true, perhaps, that the people in the churches have forgotten how to think?). But we must not believe that God condemns the intellect. I am not trying to defend intellect; I am making this comment so that we can have an accurate grasp of the situation: "Do not be conformed to the present age, but be transformed by the renewing of the mind, so that you may discern what the will of God is . . ." (Rom 12:2), and likewise, "it is in Jesus . . . that you have been taught . . . to be renewed in the spirit of your mind . . ." (Eph 4:21–23). It would be easy to cite additional texts. These ones are adequate to demonstrate that:

1. Faith produces a renewing of the mind. But what can this mean if not a transformation in understanding, in how to consider things, even in reasoning itself? Christian intellectuals can no longer have, I do not say the same philosophy, but certainly the same understanding of things and the world, their reality, and the human person. They can no longer conceive of them in the same way, see them in the same light. But what does this mean in practical terms? This is what all Christian intellectuals must strive to determine in their work.[4]

2. This transformation has to do with the present age. It is a point of separation with this era—and appears to be the decisive place where this separation occurs. Since matters can no longer be understood in

---

than to immediate, practical application.

4. In the 1950s, Ellul helped to organize and lead various associations of Protestant professionals in banking, medicine, and other fields—vocational affinity groups in which one could reflect on what it meant to be a Christian (salt of the earth, light of the world) in that particular field. See Ellul, *In Season, Out of Season*, 62–67. (DG)

the same way and the mind is transformed, conformity with the present age is broken. This reveals the crucial role that intellectuals have as teachers in the church. Here perhaps we have the role of doctors . . . .[5]

3. This transformation comes about through Jesus Christ and the action of the Holy Spirit. It is not a purely intellectual process, then (and this is what I meant when I said that it is not a matter of some other philosophy), but a transformation of life that is intellectually expressed. It is the Holy Spirit who animates our mind from now on, enabling us to discover new ways of thinking and a new understanding of the world we are living in.

4. This transformation has as its ultimate purpose the discerning of God's will—particularly in the area of ethics, because our text speaks to us of what is "good, agreeable, and perfect."[6] It is concerned with understanding God's will for the world, which is active in people's midst, not God's abstract or general will or his essence. And it is also concerned with what human beings can and must do in this world in order to live according to God's will.

1

In the sphere of intellectual life, the major fact of our time is a kind of unconscious but widely shared refusal to grasp the real situation that the world reveals. People refuse to see what truly constitutes our world. While this is especially true of intellectuals, it is also true of all people of our day and of our civilization as a whole. It is as though an enormous machine had been designed to keep people from becoming aware, to propel them into unconscious rejection or a flight into unreality. The grave characteristic of this era on this level is that people no longer grasp anything but appearances. They believe in appearances, they live within them, and they die for them. Reality disappears, the reality of people in themselves and the actual things surrounding them.

The people of the twentieth century—and it can be said that this is the first time in history that this situation has occurred—vacillate continuously between the phenomenon and the explanatory myth, that is, between

---

5. *Doctor* in the sense of teacher. The word in Latin means *educated person*.

6. Rom 12:2.

two extreme and conflicting appearances. The phenomenon, let us say, is the external presentation of some fact. Our contemporaries see only representations of the fact, which the press, radio, television, propaganda, and advertising provide. They no longer have faith in their own experiences, judgment, and thinking. They rely on printed paper, sound waves, or televised images. In their eyes, a fact becomes true when the newspaper prints an account of it, and they judge its importance by how tall the headline is. What they have seen for themselves does not count unless it is officially communicated and crowds have given it credence.

This observation may appear simplistic, but it is in fact how all propaganda works.[7] A fact is false. It gets printed in a newspaper in a million copies. A thousand people know it is false. But nine hundred and ninety-nine thousand believe it is true. This is what I mean by phenomena or appearances, which modern people latch on to and comprehend *exclusively*. Why exclusively? Because each day they have a very small number of actual experiences, and most of the time they behave so much by habit that they do not even notice them. By contrast, each day they learn a thousand pieces of news from their newspaper, TV, and radio, and these matters are very important and sensational! How can you expect their pathetic, individual experiences about [such mundane matters as] the excellence of a plum or a razor blade not to be drowned in such a flood of illusions, on such important topics as nuclear armament, the fate of Europe or North-South relations, strikes, and so on? Yet they will never actually gain true knowledge of these facts.

Such appearances therefore become their life and thought. This means something very important from the intellectual point of view, which is that modern people, caught up in this flood of images that they cannot verify, are in no way capable of mastering them, because these images lack all coordination. One item of news follows another without pause. An issue appears and then disappears from the newspaper columns or screen and from the reader's brain. It is replaced by other issues and is forgotten. People get used to living in this way, without a present or a past, in complete incoherence. All their mental activity is caught up in these fleeting visions, which themselves have no past or future and only an unstable present.

7. Ellul wrote a major sociological work titled *Propaganda: The Formation of Men's Attitudes* (the subtitle was added only to the English translation) as well as a brief *Histoire de la propagande*. His *The Humiliation of the Word* brings together sociological and theological perspectives on communication, truth, and reality in one of Ellul's great works. (DG)

Within this reality, the actual facts that are available to everyone remain entirely hidden. Since they are not presented as appearances, they must not exist. So, social classes (except for the dictatorship of class!), large cities, and public transit systems (except for questions of urbanism!) [do not exist]. Attention is drawn to facts that have no deep importance and constitute trivial news items,[8] about politics, the military, the economy, the democratic system, the success of the red army or the blue army, the United Nations, or nationalizations and privatizations.[9] Through the appearance that we grant them, all these trivial details are where people focus their passions.

Yet people obviously need some degree of coherence. They cannot reconcile themselves to being just an unmoving eye that registers impassively all of the disjointed and random images of a crazy kaleidoscope. They need sensible connections and coherence for all of these fleeting facts. This cannot be the facts' true coherence, however, because that would require a true understanding of them rather than our superficial view, as well as a prodigiously sharp and far-reaching mind. So as the means of communication and propaganda develop and as the proportion of intellectuals to others declines, the more necessary it becomes to simplify, to summarize these news items and this phenomenology.[10] The more urgent it becomes to provide the explanation and connection for all this trivial news. But the explanation and connection must be at the level of the "average reader," a level that is automatically getting lower and lower.

This brings us to the other pole of our bizarre intellectual situation today: the explanatory myth. In addition to its political and its mystical and spiritual function, the explanatory myth is the veritable spinal column of our whole intellectual system. It was thought to be inessential, connected with dictatorial regimes, but in fact it forms an essential part of every contemporary kind of politics in our context. Given that appearances produce confusion and coherence is needed, a new appearance unifies them all in the viewer's mind and enables everything to be explained. This appearance has a spiritual root and is accepted only by completely blind credulity. It becomes the intellectual key for opening all secrets, interpreting every fact,

8. *Faits divers*, varied facts or happenings. A section of the newspaper containing brief, sensational articles.

9. The Red Army was the name of the Russian or Soviet army between 1918 and 1946. The blue army is presumably the US army.

10. That is, this immersion in appearances rather than reality.

and recognizing oneself in the whirl of phenomena. We are all familiar with these explanatory myths: the bourgeois myth of the hand of Moscow, the socialist myth of the 200 families, the fascist myth of the Jews, the communist myth of the anti-revolutionary saboteur, and so forth and so on.[11] But what is obviously very serious is that human beings today no longer possess any other means of intellectual coherence and political inquiry than this myth. If they dispense with it, they can retreat from the world they live in and lead their individual lives, but that is a suicidal way out, because they cannot isolate themselves from the world as we have constructed it.

This myth, which we are not seeking to fully analyze here, is also for our contemporaries their one stable point of thought and consciousness. It provides understanding and coherence and also seems to be the one fixed element amid the swirl of facts. This enables everyone to avoid the trouble of thinking for themselves, the worry of doubt, the questioning, the uncertainty of understanding, and the torture of a bad conscience. What prodigious savings of time and means, which can be put usefully to work manufacturing some more missiles! People of our day have a good conscience because they have an answer for everything; and whatever happens and whatever they do, they can rely on the explanation that myth provides. This process places them within the most complete unreality possible. They live in a permanent dream, but a realistic dream, constructed from the countless facts and theories that they believe in with all the power of "mass persons" who cannot detach themselves from the mass without dying.

* * *

How did this situation arise, which it seems impossible to escape? A whole assortment of facts contributes to the explanation. In the first place, there is our world's real, extraordinary complexity. The more we go forward, the more our world is constructed of complicated organizations that are interlocking, with various properties, and all seeming of equal importance. It is impossible to understand them, to grasp them as a whole. We wander aimlessly in this forest.

---

11. These conspiracy theories referred, respectively, to the belief that the Soviet government influenced the internal affairs of other countries, that 200 families by their wealth controlled France's economy and political life, that Jews were communists (or simply enemies), and that saboteurs were obstructing the advance of communism.

Then there is the influence of the means of knowledge that are available for encountering these facts. These media are essentially mechanical in nature. And because they require considerable capital for their operation, they necessarily rely on private or state capital. These two characteristics of the means have political or economic repercussions: their mechanical nature requires that they be devoted only to the externality of facts. There are "some things that can be produced on TV, and some things that cannot." We can understand them from one angle only.

This double condition leads as a result to a mechanical choice in the actual data. We have to look for what fits the means' requirements. In the end, the mechanical nature makes it necessary to use massive and unqualified assertions—assertions rather than reasoning, because, due to the fact that it is mechanized, we are addressing the crowd. Since the means are subservient to money, they give preference to the spread of some facts over others, they present one aspect of the world based on hidden assumptions. The means are progressively applied in all areas and to everyone, because the business needs a good return (financially so, if it concerns "private information," politically so, if it concerns "information of state"—it is the same thing either way).

A third element in the explanation comes from the overwhelming nature of the means of knowledge that society makes available to us. We find it difficult to deny information that comes to us in this manner—and even if we have private doubts, this does not keep the crowd from accepting the information, due to how forceful it appears. There can be no dialogue with the media. Their mass power is completely irresistible when used under certain conditions (which special research centers are dedicated to determining more and more precisely).

Finally, we must obviously take into account entertainment, in the Pascalian sense of the word.[12] Every person today is a person for civilization to entertain, and it could be said that our entire civilization, from its pastimes right up to its serious issues, looks on everything from the perspective of entertainment. This is what I meant when I spoke of "keeping people from becoming aware." Lifestyle, activities, work, political parties, and so on—all this is so absorbing that people become easier prey for these means of knowledge. These means are reinforced by those who use

12. In his *Pensées* (Thoughts), Blaise Pascal (1623–62) noted that people pursue *divertissements*, diversions or distractions, in order to avoid becoming aware of their existential unhappiness.

them, since people are profoundly incapable of deep thought and reflection. These phenomena, these obvious explanations satisfy them, because they are entertained, even before the information from film and radio has entertained them a bit more. The intellectual situation of modern people is therefore extremely serious. Although they know more things, have more means, and are theoretically more advanced than at any other period in history, they are advanced in a dream of explanations and a fog of facts.

* * *

One would think, though, that this is not the modern intellectual's situation. It may be the situation of the average person and that is all. In fact, intellectuals are entirely caught up in it, albeit in a different way.

Intellectuals are able to penetrate the nullity of the explanatory myths quite easily, and they can reject them and leave behind the disturbing "simplism" that is today's wretched dogmatism. But having put these aside, they are still completely unequipped to face the mass of news items that come at them from all sides. They are quite able to challenge the myth, but they are not able to grasp reality. So, in the current intellectual system that rotates on an axis passing through two poles, "phenomenon" and "myth," they have to retain one of these poles, the phenomenon, and this produces a complete disequilibrium in their thought. They have to stop here, because they have no control over the phenomenon. These intellectuals know perfectly well, however, that it is just an appearance. They can be completely clear about the unreality of what others believe to be facts. But they cannot grasp this reality any more than others can.

What will they do? For some, the way out is suicide: they close their eyes and adopt the myth so that they can stay connected to people in general. They obey this sophism: "The phenomenon and the myth do not correspond to facts, of course, but since people believe them, they become reality, and that is the reality we need to deal with." This is the great paradox of communist or fascist intellectuals (it is true that there are not many in this camp!).[13] This is the suicide of intellectual awareness and clarity in order to find a reason for being. So intellectuals disguise their suicide with

---

13. A paradox, that is, because while these intellectuals believe in the study of reality through reason, they must admit the importance of irrational and emotional constructions of reality.

a spurious crown of laurels, by, for example, referring to the myth that they have adopted as "human permanence" or "historical dialectic."

Others commit suicide another way. Since the phenomenon is so overwhelming and invasive, it becomes impossible to have an accurate picture of the political, social, and human reality of our day. People move along so completely in the midst of appearances. When people realize this, they despair of ever being able to know anything differently and finding any coherence whatsoever within this perpetual flux. So intellectuals increasingly come to believe that there is no reality behind the appearances, or that, if one exists, it is impossible to grasp and holds no meaning for human beings. From then on, there is no point in searching for explanation and coherence, because we are wandering in the midst of shadows. And because everything is conveyed to our understanding under the form of appearance, because everything is already interpreted, intellectuals refuse to hold any fact as valid and sure, since they know that they cannot verify the reality of any of them. As a result, awareness of the world they are in slips away from them. This takes on various forms, such as desperate heroism or surrealistic dilettantism. But in each case, it is an intellectual suicide resulting from despair over their actual situation.

No matter how we look at it, all modern intellectuals adopt one or other of these positions. This is particularly obvious with the so-called Parisian intelligentsia. The intellectual's situation is therefore not an especially enviable one. Today it is more precarious than ever, since there are so many "career prospects," and novelists make fortunes (yes, but look at those who do!), and there is such high demand for educated and technically oriented people. This precariousness no longer relates to material conditions but to the very intellectual and spiritual conditions in which intellectual occupations are carried out. In other words, intellectuals are endangered from within and no longer from without. This is not exactly a good place to end [this analysis].

We have considered one of the aspects of the intellectual transformation of our day; there is another that is just as grave.

* * *

Until the present day, intellect had various modes of expression and ways of influencing the world and the people in it. In our day, intellect has found a mode of expression that corresponds to our civilization and that presents some new and disturbing features. This mode is technique. Technique has overtaken the realm of intellect just as it has every other realm of activity. Of course, this term *technique* must be taken in its broadest sense; we can envision technique that is literary (more thoroughgoing than it has ever been: in Faulkner, for example), sociological, legal, and historical, not only scientific.[14] In fact, technicians exploit every intellectual field. This has the advantages, of course, that technique always offers: precision, speed, security, progress, and universality—all the characteristics of efficiency.

This is not to say that technique is anti-intellectual. We could easily state the opposite: that intellect has become technique. It is useless to deplore this situation, but it is important to understand it. Technique is, here as elsewhere, a tool placed at intellect's disposal. But after our study of end and means, this should hardly be reassuring, since it is indeed the case that this tool has effects on the modern intellect that are quite corrosive.

What is striking is that technique seems to be our intellect's one irrefutable instrument. Whether it is a matter of intellectual approach, influence on the world, or self-reflection—for every intellectual operation there is a technical route, and because it is faster, more effective, and more practical, it is the one route that modern intellectuals can follow. There is no longer a choice. An entomologist will no longer proceed like Fabre, or a historian like Commynes.[15] Precise techniques exist that give much better results—and if people do not use them, they are considered amateurs or even fools. It could be said in fact that technique is today the sole route that intellect uses to truly express itself. This can be seen of course in art, either directly as in cinema, or indirectly as in modern painting (which in fact is conditioned by its obsession to stake out ground and differentiate itself from photography: a technical problem).

Now, this instrument—which intellect can modify, bend, and apparently dominate—in fact produces profound changes in intellectual behavior, because it excludes every other instrument. It becomes imperious. That intellect can be expressed through intuition is affirmed in the abstract, but it cannot be reconciled with this remarkably precise tool. We can grasp this imperialism of technique by, for example, our modern intellectuals' attitude toward ways of knowing and doing that follow other

14. William Faulkner (1897–1962), writer.

15. While Jean-Henri Fabre (1823–1915) is considered a founder of entomology and Philippe de Commynes (1447–1511) the first modern historian, each followed an idiosyncratic method or style that has been surpassed by today's "precise techniques."

methods, such as those of Indians or Tibetans. Modern intellectuals view such methods as objects for sociological study but not as a way still open that may reveal actual knowledge of what is true. Only some lunatics, generally Anglo-Saxons, mystically pursue these routes.[16] And it is obvious that such modes of knowledge could not in any way compete with our technique. This is just one example.

To the very degree that intellect is tied to its technical expression and intellectuals tend to become technicians, their scope of action becomes singularly restricted although its technical possibilities seem to increase. Because intellect cannot detach itself from its instrument, it remains restricted today to the sphere in which this tool can operate and be used.

If we look at the matter fairly, we have to acknowledge that current opinion recognizes "serious intellectualism," which relates to what can be used (technique), and an intellectualism of fantasy, which is not taken seriously and has no impact in any sphere. It cannot become technique, because its object is inadequate to the technical method. Theology is an example, as is metaphysics, and, generally speaking, art.

This is nothing but intellect's confinement to its one modern method. Intellect is condemned to acting upon only what can be seen, weighed, counted, or measured. It functions within the strict sphere of the material world and tends to deny the other world. What used to be considered a materialist theory is today a result of intellect's very method. This is more serious, because a doctrine can be refuted, but technical method cannot be called into question. The intelligence of modern human beings ceases to be nourished by the springs of contemplation and awareness. It aligns itself more and more with the data of its created instrument—the tool that has as its primary object the modification of the material world.

Thus, intellectuals who take their work seriously can no longer be anything but materialists, not because of doctrine but because of the very methods they use. If they hold some other philosophical position it will have no effect on their work, at least not in terms that call their technique into question. That would obviously be catastrophic, not from the authentic intellectual point of view but from that of their individual careers (because such intellectuals would cease to be taken seriously).

As for those who claim that they remain truly spiritualist, humanist, and so on while making use of rational technique, their lack of clarity

---

16. When used in French, *Anglo-Saxon* refers to contemporary English-speaking people and their civilization.

demonstrates that they are not real intellectuals. Action that is completely oriented toward the material world and no longer takes account of the spiritual elements is, in the final analysis, necessarily destructive of this spiritual reality at the heart of intellect. Intellect has become increasingly enslaved to its method and seems no longer able to find an escape route. What should be intellect's liberation is the worst slavery that it has ever known. Freed from dogmas, it is enslaved to means. There is no more struggle and tension between Ariel and Caliban. Caliban has perfected a system in which the shackled Ariel finds his reason for being and strokes his chains with delight, in the illusion of a power that is actually Caliban's very own.[17]

There have been reactions of course, sometimes violent ones. Cubism and surrealism were reactions, which tried to find through intellect a position to take in the world apart from technique. But what vitiates these reactions is that such movements deny the existence of a reality other than the apparent phenomena and reject an objective reality. We come down again to the first element of intellectual degradation today. Besides, as soon as an explosion gives birth to such movements, they must become concerned with their effectiveness, and so they have bowed to the current law and hared off in pursuit of new techniques. The fact is striking with regard to surrealism and its partisan quarrels.[18] It is apparent that strict rules are applied, which may appear in different guises but which are the same in basic features. These strict rules are in fact technical rules, and they exclude intellectual freedom.

* * *

These two facts that I have just emphasized, the failure of awareness and the subjugation of intellect to technique, lead in combination to the most frightening situation possible for an intellectual: the absence of communication.

It is a banal observation that the people of our day no longer understand one another. This has not been news since the tower of Babel. But God did preserve to people a certain degree of relationship, thanks to intellect.

17. Characters in *The Tempest*, a play by William Shakespeare (1564–1616). For Ellul's purpose here, Ariel represents the spiritual and Caliban the material reality.

18. The movement split into two groups, each claiming title to the name of surrealism and producing its own manifesto of the movement's meaning and aims. The group lead by André Breton (1896–1966) gained ascendancy and continued to undertake various "purges" of its members.

This is the bridge that our day has just destroyed. Human beings no longer understand one another. At the peasant's level, it is not noticeable; at the bourgeois level, it is an inconvenience. But at the intellectual's level, it is a tragedy, because for intellectuals there is no real reason to live except for communicating, for understanding the world.[19] Today, however, such communication has become practically impossible. In order for people to understand each other they need a minimum of shared true ideas, biases, and values, which are usually held unconsciously.

Yet the mechanics of information progressively destroys this common fund. Other biases are probably created, other shared ideas, but they have other characteristics. Instead of being the deepest and most authentic expression of a particular civilization, they are now the myths and artificial ideas created by propaganda. That is, individuals can no longer encounter one another themselves, along a given civilizational path; they can encounter in each person only the myth that they themselves believe. And this myth is only an *artificial* creation (we must keep returning to this point) that keeps modern people from descending into madness.

Besides, we have seen how the sense of objective reality becomes gradually lost and also how the people whom we encounter have ceased to hold for us this objective reality. We are caught up in this increasingly greater abstraction that is occurring in relation not only to facts but also to human beings. We can no longer communicate with one another because our neighbors have ceased to be real to us. Intellectuals today no longer believe in the possibility of joining with others. They speak into the void and for the wasteland, or else they speak for the proletariat, the Nazi, the intellectual, and so on. People have never spoken so much about human beings while at the same time giving up speaking to them. And this is because they are well acquainted with how useless it is to speak to them: conditions are such that the human person has disappeared. What remains is the consumer, the worker, the citizen, the reader, the partisan, the producer, the bourgeois. What remains are those who tricolor and those who internationalize.[20] In all this, the person has disappeared, and yet it is only to the human person

---

19. We should not infer that Ellul ranked occupations or groups in society as having greater or lesser worth. Ellul is considering here the role of language in the work that is done by manual laborers, business people, and those who, as stated in an earlier footnote, "read, think, discuss, write, and teach about truth and reality."

20. That is, those who are nationalists (the French flag has three colors) and those who are internationalists.

that we can speak authentically. It is only with the human person that we can communicate.

In the end, we can no longer communicate with people because the sole way of intellectual expression is technique. This fact, that intellect has to follow the channel of technique, leads to the destruction of personal relationships because there is no possibility of contact between two beings this way. [Real] communication transcends technique, because it cannot occur unless the two interlocutors are completely engaged in real discussion. But this is precisely what modern intellectual technique both avoids and frustrates.

Now, modern intellectuals realize this enormous impossibility—it is their very condition that is in jeopardy. In the final analysis, it is a question of knowing whether they still have something to say to another that the other can hear—instead of holding forth indefinitely (or acting, which amounts to the same thing) on the topic, and improving the means [of communication]. And this also concerns intellectuals who call themselves Christian. So modern intellectuals seek various paths. De Rougemont goes looking for engaged thought, or Malraux rediscovers the human person in the Event, and so on.[21] Such paths are not false, but they are useless, because if we say that human beings can be rediscovered in the Event, for example in war, revolution, or concentration camps, this means that they can be rediscovered only in exceptional situations, outrageously costly for our civilization, and only to the very extent that they escape from these situations. Such efforts do not get to the crux of the problem, because they necessarily fall within a temporary, limited, and inconstant sphere. [By contrast,] the physical or spiritual venture that is so needed for communication to become possible again is itself nothing other than the expression of this communication as already real. What has been broken cannot be reassembled from the outside. It is impossible to recover the human being artificially and in what is exceptional. Our entire civilization must be called into question—and everyone must participate, at the level of their individual destinies, which may not be heroic but which are assuredly the destinies of human beings, who cannot go without authentic communication with those around them.

21. Denis de Rougemont (1906–85) urged that thought and action should be united; one should not be merely an armchair philosopher. *Pensée engagée* (Engaged Thought) was the title of a regular column in the journal *Esprit*. In the novels of André Malraux (1901–86), characters take action in wars, concentration camps, and other extreme circumstances and thereby create or reveal the human condition.

Here we again put our finger on one of the wills to death of our time, one of the forms of universal suicide that Satan is slowly drawing people toward. Satan habituates them little by little to the idea of it. Suicide through pleasure or despair, intellectual or moral suicide—people then become ready for the total suicide that is slowly being readied and that will involve, body and soul, the entire world.

We must stand against this habituation to suicide in all its forms. The form of non-communication is particularly pernicious and invisible, because the people of our day put their confidence for meeting one another in the postal system,[22] railways, and television—which is to say, precisely in what crushes and destroys the very power of meeting each other in one's bodily reality.

* * *

> I call heaven and earth as witnesses today against you: I have set before you life and death, blessing and curse. Choose life, that both you and your descendants may live, to love the Lord your God .... (Deut 30:15–20)

> We give you thanks, O Lord God Almighty, who is and was, because you have taken your great power and entered into your reign. The nations were in revolt, but your wrath has come—and the time has come to judge the dead—to recompense your servants, prophets, saints, those who fear your name, small and great, and *to destroy those who destroy the earth.* (Rev 11:17–18)

2

It is clearly artificial to say that we have found solutions in a correct theology. It is not by applying principles or intellectual knowledge that we will put an end to this impossible situation of intellectuals, torn between their mission and their means, between their knowledge and the absence of communication. What can succeed is not a human action—it is, again, a question of life—nor is the problem of how intellect may be incarnated gratuitous and superfluous. It is essential for our time, but only through a superhuman action will this human effort be able to take its meaning.

---

22. *P.T.T., Postes, télégraphes et téléphones,* the French telecommunications company.

In all that follows, we will come up against a logical impossibility. We will come up against territory that is reserved to God. We will come up against the fact that all human action becomes effective only when it is filled with the fullness that God supplies—becomes complete only if God provides its completion.

This may be a good time to clear up some confusion that may have arisen in reading the first two chapters. We should not think that relations between God and human beings, concerning this needed action, are formed as though people do their part of the work and God does the rest ("God helps those who help themselves"). In reality, human beings do their work and God supplies to that work his meaning, value, effectiveness, influence, truth, justice—his life. And if God does not supply these things, let us not delude ourselves; let us not hope that human beings' work will still retain a modicum of value and truth. Nothing remains of the work of human beings. It is only a work of death; it enters into nothingness.

This is why, in all that I have said about this necessary work in our present-day civilization, there is the breach that cannot be filled in, the underground work that cannot be evaded, through which God's power is manifested (or not).[23] Our action is necessary, but useless if God does not transform it through the unpredictable and gratuitous gift of his grace.

To claim to give human beings any means and solutions that do not include this breach, to do works that supply their own effectiveness, is to do anti-Christian work, even if it takes its inspiration from the gospel. Of course, our position leaves human beings with their thirst unsatisfied. But this is because they refuse to quench their thirst with living water, of which it is said that "whoever drinks of it will never thirst again."[24] This dilemma will appear even more evident here.

* * *

The first duty of Christian intellectuals today is the duty to become aware. It is, in other words, the duty to understand the world and ourselves, inseparably linked and inseparably convicted, in their reality. It means rejecting appearances, information for the sake of information, the abstract

---

23. The images here of breach and underground work (literally, *sapping*) depict operations of trench warfare.

24. John 4:14.

phenomenon, the reassuring illusion of progress, and the belief that people and situations can be improved through a kind of good historical fate.

The first act, the first necessity for becoming aware, is a ferocious and passionate destruction of myths, intellectual idols, unconscious rejections of reality, and outmoded and empty doctrines (such as liberalism, fascism, or communism in the political sphere). It means overthrowing this intellectual bourgeois spirit of conformist thinking, either to a dogma (as in Russia) or to a way of life (as in the United States). It means a violent break with the carnival of news programs and trivial news reports, and a puncturing, through careful analysis, of the interpretations and trial balloons on offer for elevating the world. But in the name of what would it be elevated?

The second element of becoming aware is the will to find the objective reality of the facts and the life that those around me lead. It means creating an authentic realism, like what I have tried to describe in the work on political realism already mentioned. But here again, we need to ask the question: In the name of what?

The third element is that this reality must be grasped first on the human level. We must strenuously refuse to detach ourselves from this terrain, which is low-lying but alone significant. This means, first, that we must avoid flight in all its guises, into the ideal, the future, the general, and the abstract. We must not think about "human beings" but about my neighbor Mario. It is in the real life, which I can easily come to know, about this particular person, that I see the true repercussions of the machine, the press, political speeches, and government. I may be told that things are different for a farmer in Texas or for a Kolkhozian,[25] but I know nothing about that (and news reports are not what will inform me), and I have my doubts, because I believe in a human nature.

I refuse to believe that humanity is making progress, when from one year to the next, among men and women I know, whose lives I observe and among whom I live, I see debased the meaning of responsibilities, the dignity of labor, the recognition of a true authority, and the concern to live honorably. When I see them weighed down by worry about what the "important people" are up to, by the fear that oozes from our world, and by the hatred of a formidable phantom that they never succeed in putting a name to. When I see them, driven by circumstances and in pain, becoming thieves, liars, embittered, miserly, selfish, faithless, and full of rejection and rancor. Or when I see them involved in a desperate struggle from the

25. A farmer on a Soviet collective farm.

depths of their hearts against what they do not understand. Intellectuals who want to do their work must today start again at the beginning: with the beings whom they know and first of all with themselves. It is at this level and no other that they must start contemplating the world's situation.

If they want to understand what the cinema is, they should go to the cinema, not to see a work of art or anything like that—but in order to dwell there. In other words, to enter into communion with the crowd of spectators, to see them instead of the film, to share their perspective and feelings. Then they will know what destructive power toward human beings the cinema contains within itself, a power that subtracts nothing from the cinema's other, positive qualities. Clearly, this awareness, which has nothing intellectual about it, needs a strong stomach—and runs the risk of producing some sleepless nights. But when intellectuals do this, then they will be on the path that leads to the true struggle for the life of intellect. All other knowledge of the world, through statistics or news, is illusory and enslaves us to the tendencies that we have discussed.

The fourth element of this awareness consists in considering contemporary problems in depth, seeing them as they are, with, on the one hand, the merciless ways of our world and, on the other hand, the situation that they present to us. It is a matter of finding, behind the facts that are projected to our view, the reality on which they are based. Thus, behind the various aspects of propaganda there is a reality that is common to all countries and states and that is propaganda itself, stripped of its affective or ideological content that has no real importance. It is a matter of finding, behind the doctrines that assault and blind us from every direction, the reality that they conceal. Thus behind the democratic or totalitarian aspects there is the reality of the technical state, which pursues its course regardless of whatever exterior form it may take. What matters is that by scouring extremely hard and carefully we uncover the true structure of our modern civilization, the expression of its spiritual reality, the present expression of the world's spiritual reality. But this civilizational awareness cannot be objective in any way. And this is the final element that awareness consists of: it must be a commitment.

Intellectuals who carry out this work absolutely cannot do it in the manner of nineteenth-century liberal intellectuals. They cannot consider themselves observers, on the sidelines, independent with regard to these objects that are human beings and society, indifferent and detached from material conditions and accommodating only their personal passions or observations. Intellectuals who want to become aware must consider themselves on the level of other human beings, along with them, subject to the same laws, influences, and despair, and destined to the same death. And it is for these people, as well as for themselves, that they must become aware, that they must wake up from this hideous nightmare in which techniques induce the world to slumber. They must consider themselves part of this world whose structures they are uncovering, incorporated into this civilization, revolving along with it, dependent on it, but also perhaps able to change it.

It is a matter of committing to this enterprise, seeing concretely what the world is, and seeing ourselves concretely within the world. This is not the time for utopias and even less for political realisms. It is the time for awareness, which engages the life of each person. For, of course, those who become committed in this way accept that their entire life becomes engaged. They enter into an authentic drama, not a figurative one. And this simply means that one cannot be a communist intellectual and store up highly profitable capital, like the type of scholar we are so familiar with, or an anarchist writer and hold substantial publishing contracts, or a proletarian poet and travel in first class. On the intellectual level, the scandal is the same as that of a Christian who manufactures weapons or finances their export. On the economic level, it is the absence of commitment in life, the absence of awareness, and the good conscience that proceeds from the illusions of the kingdom of Satan.

But again, in what name do we say and do these things? How can we bring about this reversal that seems so impossible? To become aware really means to recover in every sphere the reality that our world is looking for. And what can we do on our own in this discussion? What can we understand about this spiritual reality that conditions material reality? (Our experience clearly shows us that it is so, but we cannot go further here.)

In short, this entire awareness can come only from the Holy Spirit. Here we arrive at the caesura. We have been able to clearly determine what is necessary, and many have been able to agree up to this point. But we have not found either the means or the reason, in other words, the motive power. And how we twist and turn! For several millennia, human beings have been drawing up the same bucket from an empty well. Whatever effort human beings have undertaken, its meaning and value have come only in Jesus Christ and by the Holy Spirit. Appearances change nothing. This assertion cannot be developed further here.

But we should at least note the extreme predicament we are in. In reality, all of our civilization's systems of interpretation and understanding are incorporated into it (including the materialist dialectic that is an integral part of this world that we might call bourgeois, and the surrealism that is an indisputable element of this world that we might call traditional!).

Nothing that this world offers us is useful for this awareness. What is needed is a truth that enlightens human intellect through a greater light. What is needed is an authority that leads people necessarily to the act of understanding. What is needed is a power that reveals to people the authenticity of the milieu in which each one is placed. All this cannot come from human beings. Throughout the centuries, people could delude themselves because they were placed in a "normal" world, not a "good" one, but one "at the right level for human beings." Now delusions are no longer possible except for the mentally ill. The very structure of this world brings us up against an inescapable choice, and intellectuals can no longer give themselves good reasons for staying just as they are. In other words, intellectual effort, just like physical effort, today has no power to bring us to this awareness. Because our civilization is radically totalitarian and escape is impossible, it becomes necessary for outside intervention to take place. But there is no longer any outside to the world. Our society absorbs all forms of intellect. Because our civilization is more than human, it becomes necessary to see that it is not constructed by "flesh and blood" but by powers, dominations, "spiritual princes."[26] But nothing in our intellectual training prepares us to see and understand this. Our intellectual means are purely materialistic and completely inadequate for such deep realization. To be quite precise, there is only the intervention of the Holy Spirit, who can transform our intellect in such a way that it will no longer be encompassed within our systems and will be adequately penetrating. Today there is no longer any other possibility. Until now, the ordinary intelligence of human beings could suffice, but when faced with our civilization all it can offer is the "best of all possible words" of Huxley's sort.

Christian intellectuals must understand the decisive nature of our era, and that if we give up this awareness that demands our total selves we betray God and the vocation that he called us to. But we also betray the world that we exist in, notwithstanding all the good will that we may bring to the resolution of social or economic problems, the devotion to various "good

26. Eph 6:12.

82

causes," the zeal for making science advance, and so on. We are no longer then anything but the blind leading the blind toward death.[27]

This awareness, the sole necessary act that Christian intellectuals must undertake today, an act that must constantly be renewed, involves three results when we consider it in its concrete reality. These results are precisely what enable us to say that this awareness, enlightened by the discernment that the Holy Spirit gives, is the answer to present problems. They are what also enable us to evaluate if the awareness that has been produced is indeed genuine. And finally, they are what demonstrate how this awareness is indeed a specifically Christian act. These results are as follows: to recover the meaning of neighbor, the meaning of the event, and the limits of the sacred. These are the results that I will sketch very briefly in the lines that follow, without claiming to study them philosophically.

1. In the final analysis, communication is broken today because intellectuals are no longer the neighbors[28] of anyone. They are no longer understood by others because they no longer have anything in common with them. No matter the extent of their concern or intellectual regard for others, people are only strangers, separate beings. It is quite evident that to become neighbors again is the duty of every Christian. But it has greater urgency for intellectuals because it is a work that, for them, justifies their very presence—since it must be aware—and also because it is now a question of discovering how. Our world by itself destroys personal relationships, but some people have also consciously and scientifically undertaken to do so. Nazis and communists have conflated the adversary with the whole idea of evil. The person before us is no longer an adversary but the expression of evil itself; the "Jew," "communist," or "plutocrat" on one side, and the "bourgeois," "saboteur," or "Trotskyite"[29] on the other side is the precise incarnation of all earthly evil. As a result, they can and must be ruthlessly killed. They are no longer human beings; they are symbols.

    In the same way, but starting from the opposite direction, the most important act on the social level is to recover the neighbor. Christianity itself leads us there. It is a result of faith. The person before us is no longer merely another human being, but a person for whom Christ

27. Matt 15:14; Luke 6:39.

28. *Le prochain*, the human being considered in relation to others. Literally, the one who is next to or beside.

29. An adherent of Marxism as interpreted by Leon Trotsky (1879–1940).

died. This attitude, which all Christians should hold as a direct implication of their faith, can be consciously defined and deliberately oriented by the Christian intellectual. It is not a simple thing to become somebody's neighbor. It requires studying what it means theologically, of course, and the theological foundation of this nearness.[30] This has already been done, and as a result I will not draw our attention to this point. But this is not an easy thing in our civilization, which, as I have already noted, is particularly oriented to the destruction of personal relationships, that is, to inhibiting this nearness. By becoming aware, intellectuals recover a ground on which it is possible to find themselves again with others: the place of encounter with reality. But the particular work of Christian intellectuals is to discover today a new language, one that enables everyone to understand one other despite the clamor of advertising, a language that enables individuals to come out of their desperate solitude and that avoids both arid rationality and subjective emotionalism. To seek out a new language that "gives a purer meaning to the words of the tribe,"[31] with all that this entails of submission to what is real (our language is totally out of step with reality!) and adaptation to different mental structures. A language that might become a living expression of the words of Paul: "I have become all things to all people. . . ."[32]

This problem of language is, for Christian intellectuals, the key problem of nearness with people. Others have felt it. Others have sought for this language but ended in a solitude still more desperate, such as the surrealists.

It is normal for human beings to be separated and estranged. But the Holy Spirit creates the communication between them and enables this separation to be broken through. Only the Holy Spirit can do it. Only he can establish this connection with one's neighbor. Only he can open eyes and ears, not only to revealed truth, but to the love of others in humility. But it is still necessary for human beings to work patiently toward what the Holy Spirit will use. If they flee for refuge to the desert, irretrievably alone in an eremitic life, they will have no neighbor, and what can the Holy Spirit do about it? If

---

30. *Proximité*, closeness in space or time.

31. From the poem "Le Tombeau d'Edgar Poe" by Stéphane Mallarmé (1842–98), describing a poet's vocation.

32. 1 Cor 9:22.

in our civilization we do not create a possible language, there is no medium for the Holy Spirit's action, there is no human means, which God always requires of his creatures in order to manifest his power. The Holy Spirit alone will give this language a meaning, truth, and effectiveness, yet it is necessary for human beings to have sought out this language. Christians no longer seek it, because they believe that relations with one's neighbor are very simple, that the situation is the same as before, that what succeeded a thousand years ago is still valid. Yet Christians have rediscovered a language several times throughout Christianity's history. Today they seem little concerned to do so. It is non-Christians who are searching for it, but to this point the Holy Spirit has not fulfilled the quest.

It is urgent for intellectual Christians to regain the meaning of their vocation along this line.[33] All the work remains to be done, but it is the only way to recover a means of understanding one another that transcends classes, formulas, and political divisions. It is the only way to break down the sociological tendencies that separate us and to recover authentic nearness in love. It is today the mode by which we can live in love, absent the deadly sentimentalism that intellectual and theological liberalism had given to the idea of neighbor. If we do not discover how, our preaching about love cannot be understood.

2. A second result of awareness points us to a second task, a second obligation of Christian intellectuals. Those who believe in the trivial news item and interpret it through myth no longer believe in the event, which is to say, in a fact's intervention in the course of life, history, and development that brings with it a modifying character, that encompasses within itself the meaning of all this past development, and that entails a significance for the future. The event is the opposite of the trivial piece of news, because it is charged with experience and grasps human beings as a whole. The event is also the opposite of the modern myth, because it carries its meaning within itself and the adherence

---

33. It must be remembered that Ellul was never an ivory-tower intellectual. He worked on a farm while participating in the Resistance against the Nazi occupation of France. He served briefly in the city administration of Bordeaux after the Liberation. He was an active lay church leader and teacher throughout his life. He devoted a great deal of time to working with young people at a juvenile "prevention club." See "With the Street Gangs," chapter nine of *In Season, Out of Season*, 117–38. (DG)

that it demands is personal and brings the individual to a personal decision.

But to believe in the event is to have a certain conception of history, such that the event can come to pass. Now, at the present time, not only do the material conditions that I have described tend to make us treat the event with complete contempt, but even the *prevailing* conceptions, of history as much as of individual life, drive us to repudiate it. When I said several times that modern people live in a dream, and that even when they *fight for their bread and butter* they do not encounter material reality but abstractions, this assertion can be expressed in another way: None of the facts that occur, in the world or in personal life, have any longer for the individual any personal or independent significance, none produce an experience and a decision, but are always presented instead as the product of a mass power, a sociological action. Yet if there is no event, faith is not possible. There is only the artificial myth. This is the attitude toward life that explains, at one and the same time, the modern success of political myths and the disaffection for the Christian faith. It is the result, on the "religious" level, of the impossibility of grasping the present world's reality.

Besides, if there is no event, neither can human beings take any personal and voluntary action in history and in their life. The only thing possible then is universal capitulation. Now the problem is twofold. We need to know if there is objectively the possibility of the event in history, and if there is an event in the life of each human being.

Recognizing the event in our world is one result of becoming aware. This effort of the Christian intellectual seems absolutely necessary for refocusing the lives of our contemporaries. But to recover the event, its meaning and significance today, is not an arbitrary task of purely intellectual construction. It is not a matter of a philosophy of the event that would have any certainty other than human reason, because [in that case] nothing could prove to us that the event actually exists [except as a mental construct]. If Christians have a particular mission here, it is because they are witnesses to an event on which all the others rest, an event that occurred in history and that occurs in our lives, an event that is in short the guarantee of the other events, personal or historical, and that renders history and life radically irreversible. This event is God's intervention in the course of this history; it is Jesus Christ. We cannot reduce it to a philosophical formula.

That is the great danger that stalks us here, because to do so would reduce this certainty to nothing. We cannot say that it is eternity that has intervened in time, or an abstract God in human beings. What is properly called the event is that the living God became incarnate in the living man, Jesus.

Beginning here and only here is it possible for intellectuals to regain this ground that is indispensable for thought and life, which is the real event. From here and only here can we call men and women to personal experience, to a rediscovery of the meaning of life and the relationship that God created between Jesus Christ and life, not only the life that is called eternal, but daily life. "For those who are outside, all things come in parables. . . . How then will you understand *all* the parables?" (Mark 4:11–13). We are tasked with understanding all of these parables in which the action of Jesus Christ is inscribed, in history and in our human lives. And it is only this understanding that can give them a meaning. It is only in Jesus Christ that we can possibly understand this wild adventure into which we are thrown, because in the midst of these shadows, he is the person, in the midst of this maelstrom of facts, he is the event, in the midst of these religions, he is the author and finisher of faith.[34] Instead of losing ourselves in vain speculations or political and social agitation of the world's sort, we have here the important and authentic task of Christian intellectuals: through this event, to restore an orientation to the world in the political, social, and other spheres, and, through this event, to enable it to find the hope that does not disappoint.

3. There is a final result of awareness that will complete this description of how urgent the work of intellectuals is for the church and the world: no one else can do this labor. *At the present time* (it has not always been thus, it is not the only possible solution in the absolute sense), only Christians have been given the authentic possibility of responding to these needs.

We have seen how intellect has become enslaved to the means of expression available to it. The problem for the liberation of intellect is to reestablish intellectual techniques. But we have seen that to the extent that intellect has only one means of expression, that which is most effective, it cannot extricate itself and act on the world in another way.

---

34. Heb 12:2.

In the end, it is not by artificially creating another means of expression that we will get there. We have also seen why.

In reality, the answer to this problem resides, however strange this may appear, in discovering the boundary between the profane and the sacred (not the *religious* or the *Christian*, but the *sacred*, approximately in the sense that Otto uses).[35] This does not consist in an artificial creation of two spheres, in a division based in reason, but in intellect's recognition that two spheres exist. It is the gradual uncovering of the boundary that exists in the facts between the two spheres. It is the fact that the intellectual act, with its modern methods of investigation, has the right to go up to the boundary of the sacred, but not beyond.

For, in a real way, it can invade the sacred. It can enslave and destroy it, and then deny it. It can violate mechanistically what is beyond its powers, which is how we are destroyed when we apply intellect to human beings and the social. We have thrown the world and human beings out of balance through our powerful technique. This occurs in the details and in the structures. We have destroyed one of the world's elements of equilibrium, by applying our intellectual instruments indiscriminately to every field. To regain the limit of the sacred, to go as far as we can in intellectual activity but to stop voluntarily when we risk entering the sacred, is one of the most important tasks of intellectual inquiry.[36]

We must not conceal from ourselves that it means a *different orientation* to inquiry. This can seem like a limitation, because it implies that we have criteria of judgment that are external and superior to intellect, that intellect is not free to do all that is possible to it. It can do all, but it must not desire all that it can do; this is the intellectual temperance that we must recover. This entails the rejection of certain means, certain interventions, for the doctor, physicist, and biologist, but also for the jurist, economist, and agronomist. It also means limitation in that intellect comes to recognize that a particular sphere must remain beyond its reach, or at least beyond the action of its technical means. Yet this is the only path open to us today for restoring

---

35. Rudolf Otto (1869–1937), theorist of religion. In *Das Heilige* (*The Idea of the Holy*), he writes of human beings' experience of God as sacred, numinous, other.

36. Ellul discusses the sacred, myth, and religion in his work on the sociology of religion, *The New Demons*. (DG)

to intellect its authentic power and for situating technique in the real world. In regaining this boundary, intellect also regains the world's reality and the possibility for renewed action. For it regains the immaterial framework of the world, and under a seeming decrease of its effectiveness it attains in truth its equilibrium, another effectiveness. It recognizes that action is possible through this spiritual architecture, action on the world. And this then opens up prodigious possibilities that our intellectual methods had concealed. It is not a matter of absorbing the sacred or acting on it intellectually. But intellect can, through ways other than techniques, find the means of influencing the material world through the sacred. This is today the only fact that can spare our intellectual system from the annihilation that it is currently preparing. Besides, I do not have many illusions about the possibilities of a material renunciation for the sake of respecting the spiritual!

Now, at the present time, only Christianity enables us to begin seeking for these limits between the profane and the sacred. What sociologists or psychologists can say is limited, limited to the human, for example, and the human considered again as an *object of science*, which is entirely inadequate. What other religions can reveal is only the sacred, and today they are outdated because on this level the situation is so complex and desperate that, here again, only an intervention of the Holy Spirit can give to human intellect enough clarity and temperance to carry out this work. It is true that in Scripture there is an entire teaching on this double sphere. And we constantly find this sphere of the sacred, in human beings and in nature, not as something religious and relating to salvation, but as constitutive of the order of the world, desired by God for its preservation. The sacred is not closer to God. It is part of the world, but it is an essential part that exists beyond the reach of our sacrilegious hands because God has disposed it thus. But to know this objectively, to find it in Scripture, is insufficient, because that does not show us the present-day application or indicate the boundary for our time. Nor does it assure us of intellect's obedience, because intellect in its foolish pride looks on everything as permissible and refuses all wisdom. Wisdom comes fully only through recognizing a higher authority, which is imposed from outside upon the human mind and which provides it with a measure and also restores its authentic function.

* * *

In summary, in the intellectual sphere, in connection with the political and social spheres, a complete overhaul of all our positions must be carried out. We must begin over. And this reconstruction cannot be the work of a single person or the exclusive work of human beings. This work is necessary, not only for intellectuals, but for everyone, because if Christians do not carry out this work they should not hold out any hope about their position in the social or political world. All that they can do there will be childish, useless, and anachronistic, just like what they are currently doing. It is depressing to see Christians embarking in all of the world's social and political boats with a radical unconsciousness of the preliminary questions, which only they would be able to face.

Christian intellectuals must undertake this enormous questioning, for the world, which is wandering in a labyrinth made by its own hands; for the church, which must finally break its readymade intellectual categories; and for the other members of the church, who must receive authentic teachings about the life of faith. The work of Christian intellectuals is not an abstract pleasure but the effective participation in the preservation of the world and the edification of the church. This is why it cannot be a matter here of just a purely gratuitous exercise. We are not called to [mental] gymnastics. Above all, it is in prayer and meditation that intellectuals will recover the wellsprings of a life of the mind, rooted in what is real.

CHAPTER FIVE

Prologue and Conclusion

In the preceding pages, we were able to provide only a brief and fragmentary account. We were not concerned to offer readymade solutions but only to open up paths for the church's renewed work. This is why these pages are both a conclusion to this study as well as a prologue to fuller efforts that would examine the problem of our civilization in all its aspects—and in its concrete repercussions for the church and Christians. But if brothers and sisters in the faith have been able to sense this problem's urgency and importance, neither my time nor theirs will have been wasted.

I fully understand that all I have written seems quite intellectual and perhaps abstract. I was not concerned, however, with philosophical games or a bookish knowledge of the world in words only. But this world is complicated, much more than those that came before. Vast understanding is required to see it from all sides. All that I have written here is in fact just a kind of synthesis of a great number of facts. Behind each of the outward assertions of my description of the world there is an experience. I could provide examples to support each one, but that would have required more leisure than today's world provides, for time is short. All of it comes from observing precise and well-known facts.

But in general we are passing through the midst of facts as shades through the kingdom of the shades.[1] Day after day, the winds drive away the datebooks, newspapers, and powers, and we glide along without a

1. In Greek mythology, *shades* are spirits of the dead, persisting in a shadowy underworld.

spiritual bone structure, without memory or judgment, following every doctrine in history's current that becomes for us a perpetual past.[2] We must stand against this tendency. We must understand the world deeply, so that we may live in it. We must regain the meaning of events and the spiritual bone structure that our contemporaries have lost. The work will be difficult, because it is unfamiliar and humble. But all has been given to us (and to us Christians only) to undertake it!

* * *

Let us start again with what is simplest. One primary factual observation that becomes evident when we consider our church and our Christian action is the radical powerlessness of evangelism. The countries of what is called Christian civilization are rapidly secularizing, and the churches are less and less heeded. At the same time, the missions of Africa or Asia are showing scant progress, and the peoples of these countries are already being driven along the downward slope without first having known the rise of Christianity.[3] The world in general no longer listens to the gospel. The Word of God no longer penetrates the reality of human lives. Men and women of our day seek other solutions and heed other promises, other kinds of good news. This is a matter that should concern and worry every aware Christian. It would be simple to pursue this description further. Why it is like this? What can we do about it?

Many people before us have asked themselves these questions. Countless answers have been given, all of which seem completely superficial to me. For it concerns nothing less than recognizing today what the devil's tactic is for neutralizing the gospel. As long as that is not placed at the center we can understand nothing. We must therefore understand the situation clearly and in depth before hoping for a response. The gospel no longer penetrates. It seems that we are before a wall. Now, when we want to get past a wall, we must either find a door or create a breach. So we must first recognize this wall in order to find out if there is a door: we must therefore explore this present world. And if there is no door (as it seems to me), we must have the necessary tools to create a breach. All of the preceding

---

2. Eph 4:14.

3. Since Ellul wrote these words, in fact the growth of Christianity in Africa and Asia has been greater than its growth in other parts of the world. (DG)

studies have been in fact a search for these tools, for what can penetrate the thickness of this wall that the gospel comes up against.

I am quite familiar with what will be said: "But what is the good of this work? Doesn't simple preaching suffice?" This so-called confidence in the efficacy of God's word is actually a lack of charity toward our contemporaries, an indifference toward their concrete situation, and to a certain extent a spiritualism that is not from God. Scripture always shows us that God takes up human beings in their practical situation, in the context of their life, and enables them to act using the means of their day, in the midst of the problems of their day. When we want to repeat what St. Irenaeus or Calvin did, we are in error and unfaithfulness. When we think about the problems of today's world according to how St. Augustine or Luther described the problems of their time, we are in error and ineffectiveness.[4] For our time raises very complicated problems; our organization is more complex than that of past centuries. So also are the questions presented to one's awareness and to the Christian faith. Human beings seem each day a bit less capable of directing their times. This is not however the right time to play John the Baptist and say, "Let us preach in the desert. It is good enough to speak before a wall, and God will cause our words to be heard."

We cannot make this genuine statement: "I planted, and God gave the increase."[5] We cannot relinquish [a situation] into God's hands ("God will open eyes, ears, and hearts") until we have struggled continuously, to the point of daybreak, as Jacob did,[6] until we have waged battle up to the limit of our strength and known the despair of failure, without which this so-called confidence in God and this orthodoxy are only hypocrisy, cowardice, and laziness. All I have written has no value unless it is understood as a call to arms, exposing which adversary must be confronted, which weapons must be used. Then, at the center of this combat, the Word can be spoken—but not otherwise. When we have truly taken seriously the concrete situation of the men and women of our day, when we have heard their cry of anguish and understood why they have no desire for our disembodied gospel, when we have participated in their physical and spiritual suffering, in their despair and hopelessness, when we have entered into solidarity with our fellow citizens and our universal church, as Moses and

---

4. Irenaeus (c. 130–202), John Calvin (1509–64), Augustine (354–430), Martin Luther (1483–1546), theologians.

5. 1 Cor 3:6.

6. Gen 32:24.

Jeremiah did with their people, as Jesus did with the wandering crowds, sheep without a shepherd[7]—then our voice will be able to proclaim the Word of God. But not before!

It is tempting God to proclaim his Word for disembodied beings, for those who are in a situation such that they cannot actually hear it. Let us meditate once more on this incisive statement: "Do not cast your pearls before the swine, in case they trample them under their feet, turn against you, and tear you to pieces" (Matt 7:6). This is the striking depiction of the relationship between the church and the world today. The church, which has received the pearls of the gospel, casts them with a pious indifference like food for the swine that we are (we, too, the good Christians!), mired down in our exclusively materialist world, overwhelmed by economic and political problems, by our personal and financial fears, our worries and their realism, and perfectly integrated into the structures of the world. And these people turn against the church. "We cannot feed ourselves on your pearls. We cannot satisfy ourselves with their luster. What would you have us do with them? They do nothing for our actual situation." (And that is true!) They then rush upon the church that has dispensed fine words and illusions, to destroy it.

They are in the wrong, because the Word of God always has worth, and if it offers them nothing today it is because they are in a false situation. It is not the Word that should change and give them something else; it is their situation. But they are in the right against the church, because it is the church that should produce this change of situation, so that the Word of God might be heard within the total human condition. The church does not have the right to limit itself to sowing its pearls. It must do the groundwork so that the swine can receive its pearls. It must not separate human beings into two categories: the swine (communists, non-conformists, wrong-thinking people, workers, etc.), to whom the gospel should not be proclaimed, and the non-swine, the morose and docile sheep that our world manufactures on an assembly line. What the church must work toward is for everyone to be placed in a situation, economic and intellectual, but also psychological and physical, such that they can actually hear this gospel, be sufficiently alive for these words to have meaning, sufficiently able to respond yes or no. The secret of their choice belongs to God; even then, a decision is necessary, and they must not be placed in conditions such that they cannot respond except as swine before pearls. No pearls before the swine! But people must

7. Matt 9:36; Mark 6:34.

cease being these swine, and that is not the work of grace, it is a human work, at the level of human beings. It is a work that is horribly difficult today, and one to which Christians are particularly called because they have a better possibility than others do of seeing the true situation of humanity, where it must lead, and what its goal is.

A revolution is needed in a world in which it has become impossible, a revolution that attacks the deep structures of a civilization in which all efforts converge toward this one goal: to transform all human beings into swine, who for this reason can no longer receive the pearls of Scripture. We must rediscover the meaning of human activity, the situation of means and ends, and their true place in the world entirely given over to the spirit of power, to dissolution, and to the pride of limitless means that absorb us without possible reserve. A new communication among human beings is needed, so that relationships that have been distorted by living conditions, classes, and prejudices may, under intellect's guidance, be re-created on a personal and vital level.

It is from here that we must start out for taking action in the world and for working toward the transformation of its material conditions. Without this, without these main themes, the work that Christians do will be only sporadic, uncoordinated, lacking deep judgment, and often contrary to the true work, despite all the good will possible. In this work it is a matter principally of avoiding two errors. The first consists in a pure and simple adoption of some position of the world, whatever seems the most conformed to the "Christian ideal." One becomes a communist, liberal, pacifist, personalist,[8] and so on, following one's own tastes and sentiments, and justifies them by trotting out a Christian verity. On the pretext of being in the world, in reality this means belonging to the world. It is no longer a presence in the world but a capitulation. It is no longer to dialogue with the world but to serve as its chorus, walk in its ways, adopt its methods, and, despite appearances, play into Satan's hands.

The other error consists in seeking out God's order for this world only in Scripture and setting it forth objectively, mapping out the picture, and being satisfied with this ideational work. It expects that through some

8. Personalism, a movement in France and beyond in the 1930s and 1940s led by Emmanuel Mounier (1905–50) and Denis de Rougemont (1906–85), sought to understand human beings as persons rather than as individuals (units in a mass) and to find a social and economic basis that was neither capitalist nor Marxist. The thought of Pope John Paul II (1920–2005) is strongly infused with personalism. One American expression is the Catholic Worker movement of Dorothy Day (1897–1980). (DG)

mysterious mimicry the world will meekly proceed to align itself with this divine order. In reality, this position is a renunciation of action in the world, despite the concrete declarations that may accompany these efforts, despite the details, perhaps, of the reforms proposed. It is no longer a presence in the world; it is counsels and doctrines. . . .[9]

In fact, what is lacking in each case is the intermediate position, this perpetual "missing link"[10] that checks our Christian action. I believe that we can find it by drawing out the implications of the idea of the actual and eschatological Lordship of Jesus Christ. We have tried in this way to demonstrate the meaning of presence in the world. But this is only one of its aspects, which we had to insist on because it seemed to us poorly known and more urgent today.

* * *

For Christianity to have an entry point in the world today, it is ultimately less important to have an economic or political theory, or even political and economic positions, than to create a new way of living. It is quite evident that the first effort occurs through faithfulness to revelation, but this faithfulness to revelation can be embodied only in this creation. And here is the "missing link." There was a medieval way of living; there was a Reformed[11] way of living in the sixteenth century, and it is indeed quite interesting to consider it in contrast to the Renaissance way of living. There was a bourgeois way of living, which no longer has any spiritual quality. There is a communist way of living. There is no longer a Christian way of living. We have no need to remain deluded: a doctrine has no power (outside of what God attributes to it) except to the extent that it forms a way of living and is adopted, believed, and received by persons whose way of living corresponds to it. Marxist thought spread so tremendously precisely because it gave a true account of the situation of the people to whom it was addressed, and because it relied heavily on a way of living, imposed by economic and social conditions. The extreme weakness of liberalism or socialism is due to their no longer corresponding to a way of living. The bourgeoisie is steadily

9. *Counsels* and *precepts* (although Ellul here says *doctrines*) are Roman Catholic terms for two types of ethical principles. For Ellul's purpose here, they represent a contrast to his own understanding of Christian ethics as a living attitude, a presence.

10. Here and in the following paragraph, Ellul uses the English words *missing link*.

11. That is, Protestant, following the teachings of John Calvin.

losing its own, and what remains of it is only an outdated tradition with no relation to reality. That of the middle classes, the "working-class elite," has only ever been a pale imitation of the bourgeoisie's. Today in fact only the working masses have a way of living, but what seems new is that instead of coming from a choice, from a creation, as at the time of the Renaissance, it is imposed on them by their lifestyle, their world, and their social position. Despite its being imposed, it is indeed a way of living in that it is original (meaning distinct from others), creative of a new mental structure and a new morality, producing an organic solidarity[12] among those who adopt it, and finally, expressing a deep agreement between the individual and the social group into which the individual is integrated.

When we become concerned for the effectiveness of the gospel's action and its need to intervene in the world, it seems that the first objective should be the creation of a way of living. For if we consider the life of the Christians of our churches, we certainly see that they are good children, good parents, good spouses, good bosses, good workers—good like good bread,[13] as Aragon would say—they have many individual virtues, but they have no way of living. Or rather, they have exactly the one that is imposed on them by sociological conditions, namely that of their social class, nation, environment, and so forth. It is their political and economic condition, no longer their spiritual condition, that influences their way of living, and as such they are overwhelming proof of the temporary and this-worldly truth of Marxism. Many Christians today are perfectly aware that this situation is intolerable and that if it continues it will result in the definitive collapse of the churches of the West. This problem of the way of living is absolutely central, insofar as it is here that the question of Christianity's integration in this world, or indeed its creative power, will play out.

This is the point where all paths converge that the church patiently tries to open up: the life of ecumenism, since the universal church should be manifested as such in the life of Christians, whatever their interests or membership in other sociological groups; the life of professional associations, since the effort to integrate one's faith in one's job leads to creating a new way of living; and the pursuit of a Christian culture, a true and concrete evangelization of the proletariat worldwide, and the discovery of a new life and new forms of parishes and ecclesiastical beliefs.

12. See note 7, p. 4.
13. From "La Valse des vingt ans," a poem by Louis Aragon (1897–1982).

To create such a way of living is both a collective and an individual effort. It is the work of individual Christians, truly working out how to embody their faith in the concrete forms of their life. It is also the work of the community of Christians, in which all these efforts that are occasionally divergent or even contradictory appear. It is actually not very important for all of these efforts to logically cohere. The formation of a way of living cannot result from a solid and clearly established doctrine, which would then just be applied. Instead, it is the work of living in faith and as a result cannot satisfy us on the governmental[14] or intellectual level. But it is there that doctrine finds its human foundation and motive power. On the other hand, it is quite evident that church organizations, and also prophets, can orient the "church's flock," through the formation of this way of living, [and since] it can give rise to new investigations, they can provide support to those who venture there.

Yet as its very name indicates, the whole of life is involved in this pursuit. It is as much a way of thinking about current political events as a way of practicing hospitality. It is as much a way of dressing and eating as it is of running a business. (On this point, our austere bourgeois should understand that questions of taste, fashion, or cooking are important for forming a way of living. But being "in style" is not enough; it is even the opposite [of what I mean]. And "choosing the best quality," as commercially [defined], has nothing to do with it!) It is as much a way of being faithful to one's spouse as of being available to one's neighbor, the stance one takes concerning current social and political trends, or decisions about one's personal use of time.

I could multiply these examples, which are only suggestions to demonstrate that absolutely everything, even the slighted details that we consider to be indifferent, must be called into question, reviewed in the light of faith, and examined from the perspective of God's glory. It is on this basis that we may be able to discover within the church a new Christian way of living—intentional and true. I will hold back from giving a specific content to these suggestions, from attempting to describe this way of living. First, because it would not correspond to anything, since there is as yet no such reality; a description of this sort would be for the present a merely intellectual view. It is enough to set this requirement before Christians. Gradually it will become fitting to help it take shape through clarifications, biblical studies, and successive acts of awareness. Next, because such a description

14. *Administrative*, referring to the role or context of government.

might too easily become a springboard for Christians who would try making it into a new law. We must keep repeating: if this way of living is not Christians' creative act, it will not correspond to anything. And finally, because present-day efforts, as I indicated earlier, are diverse and uncoordinated, and it is not suitable to arbitrarily synthesize them without regard for their respective truths.

But a very important truth can be pointed out along this path, which is that such investigation is necessarily an act of solidarity. It is impossible for an isolated Christian to start out along this path. I believe that one of the essential conditions for bringing it into being is the substitution of a true solidarity among Christians (one that is created willingly through obedience to God's will) for a sociological solidarity, which is purely mechanical, which people keep harping on and want to establish as the basis for the new world. To undertake this investigation into a way of living, all Christians must feel and know that they have the support of others. And this [is needed] not only for spiritual and ideological reasons, because, for example, the problems that our world presents to human beings are difficult, but still more for reasons that are purely material. For a manual laborer or low-paid employee, for example, the question of what choice to make in their manner of life or in their occupation presents itself immediately in monetary terms. As long as solidarity among Christians does not translate into help that enables each one to find a balance in life, to seek a way of living in which their faith is truly embodied (and not to avoid dying of hunger), it will be only a word. And this just demonstrates to what point this investigation can lead into paths that are disagreeable to our fond habits. It will actually be quite disagreeable. But this is the price by which the good news of salvation in Christ will be something other than one human word among other human words. . . .

* * *

That it is, besides, clearly necessary to begin a work of rebuilding parishes and discovering Christian communities, that it is necessary to learn afresh what the fruits of the Spirit are (which are not the same as virtues), that it is necessary to recover the concrete application of temperance, freedom, unity . . . [all this] is essential for the life of the church and for presence in the world. And all this must be oriented to the preaching and proclamation of the gospel. But that is another aspect of this same work of presence in the world, another aspect that is much better known, if not in its content, at least in its necessity. That is why we do not need to investigate its principal data or trace its main themes here.

But before concluding, there is one more step to take. We have continuously tried to show how God's action, through Christians, could resolve the world's problems. How Christians, placed by God in this situation, can respond to it. But they absolutely must not get caught up in it, because what menaces the church in this necessary struggle is to become a sociological trend by taking itself seriously and wanting to take on by itself the weight of the whole effort. Then the church becomes included among the movements of the world. It becomes nationalist when the power of nationalisms arises. It becomes Bergsonian when the world offers it this exit from rationalism.[15] It becomes authoritarian when governments and the world's thoughts each turn toward authoritarianism. It comes out in favor of communities when the fashion for communitarianism transports it, and it favors colonialism when the world favors it. When the world ceases to do so, it follows suit. And now we see it being socialist or communist, because we are witnessing the apparent victory of the "left" in Europe. When it is this, it ceases precisely to be the church present in the world. In each of these cases, of course, there are theological justifications always ready to hand, because the nations are desired by God, and colonization does serve the preaching of the gospel, or indeed social justice is an authentic expression of God's justice. But these are only justifications, despite the theological truth that they contain. For when the church behaves in these ways, it stops being salt, light, and sheep. It is no longer anything but one of the forms in which the world's will is expressed, helping it in fact to attain its own ends. It no longer represents the power of God's action in the world.

It is clearly not a question of cutting the church off entirely from the world's currents. First, since it is composed of men and women living in their day, it cannot disregard these efforts and attempts, each of which presents one part of truth. It must concern itself with them, because it is not yet in heaven. But the church must be aware of them. When it undergoes the temptation of socialism, for example, it needs to understand that this does not come from God but from the world and it is a compromise, probably inevitable. It holds a certain value, but the church has neither chosen nor created this value, and its justification carries little weight. It must also

---

15. The philosopher Henri-Louis Bergson (1859–1941) taught that reality is understood through intuition and experience.

understand that these compromises almost always go poorly for the church and, *as a result,* for the world.

The church enslaved by its compromise with the state, under Constantine or Louis XIV.[16]

The church broken apart by its compromise with capitalism in the nineteenth century.

The church deprived of revealed truth by its compromise with science, in the same era.

Three examples. It would be simple to find others.

In the face of these compromises, the church must not justify itself or justify the world's solution but find the independent path that God has given it and that alone it can follow. It is only on this condition that compromise ceases to be dangerous, that the church ceases to be a sociological tendency, and that it can be present in the world with the effectiveness that the Spirit gives it. "Teach me your way, Lord. Lead me in the path of uprightness, because of my enemies. Do not deliver me to the pleasure of my adversaries. . . . Oh, if I were not sure that I would see the goodness of the Lord in the land of the living!" (Ps 27:11–13). The church's enemies seek to turn it from its proper way, to enlist it in their way, and then it becomes the plaything of the world's powers. It is delivered over to the pleasure of its adversaries. It can only take recourse in prayer to God, that he may teach it his way, which no one else can do. And this does not concern only the way of eternal salvation but the way to follow in the land of the living. The way that is truly impossible to find if God does not reveal it, truly impossible to follow with our human powers alone. And it is the same problem in the social sphere and in the individual sphere.

This way of the church in the world is, to human sight, folly, utopia, ineffectiveness, and we are seized by discouragement when we see what there really is to do in this real world. We could let everything go "if we were not sure that we would see the goodness of the Lord in the land of the living." But we have seen this goodness. It has made itself manifest, and on this foundation we can go and face the powers of the world, in our absurd powerlessness, because "in all these things we are more than conquerors, through him who loved us. For I have the assurance that neither death, nor life, nor angels, nor dominations, nor things present, nor the things

16. Louis XIV (1638–1715), French king who consolidated the state's influence over the church.

101

to come, nor powers, nor height, nor depth, nor any other creature, will be able to separate us from the love of God, manifested in Jesus Christ our Lord!" (Rom 8:37–39).

Afterword: Notes on Revolution

At the time that the 1989 English edition was being prepared, Ellul provided two extensive notes and identified the places where they belonged in his text. They were printed as an appendix to that edition.

NOTE 1

Footnote 6 on page 20 indicates the point where this note belongs.

Since the time that this book was written, there have been immense revolutionary movements. I think I can classify them into three groups: movements of struggle against an occupying colonial power, generally associated with a revolutionary will; revolutionary movements related to the Cultural Revolution in China (everything associated with 1968 and the following years); and then, Islam.[1]

As for the first kind, they present nothing new. The will to be free is nothing more or less than Third World people's adherence to a Western creation: nationalism. Strictly speaking, there is nothing here that is revolutionary in relation to Western civilization. As for the revolutionary ideology that many people have made such a noise about, it is nothing other than communism. It is communism with an African or Amerindian flavor, but it can be subjected to the same critique that we directed toward the

---

1. The Cultural Revolution, instigated by Mao Zedong (1893–1976), occurred from 1966 to 1976 and created profound upheaval, suffering, and change in Chinese society. *Everything associated with 1968* refers to protests, strikes, uprisings, and other forms of political action that occurred in France and other countries in that year.

communist ideology: nothing essential changes in the course of our society, which is now worldwide (state and technique).

The movements that have come out of the Cultural Revolution have seemed much more revolutionary in fact. In China, there was the destruction of the traditional social structure and the culture of the entire people, the complete rejection of Western techniques, the will to create a new political organization, and the replacement of techniques by the number of workers. It was true reversal, true revolution. But in the Americas and Europe, these movements of 1968 were slow to develop and failed to put anything in motion, even a lasting political movement. As for China, it is a perfect example: after six years of Cultural Revolution that destroyed families, villages, and traditions, failure had to be recognized on every level. And the Great Helmsman was a dictator.[2] Since then—and this is the fundamental point—China has returned to the path of technique, productivity, economism. In other words, revolution has been conquered by technique.

By contrast, Islam poses the same problem, but more fully and to this point more successfully. It is the only power today that calls the worldwide structures into question, and we understand why Garaudy, for example, viewed it as the sole revolutionary force capable of combatting all the vices of the modern world.[3] Islam has reinitiated its conquest of the world, and this is a true revolution because Islam denies the modern state (since it holds that the state and religion must be one reality) and because it completely rejects technique, or the Western-style technical system, in order to return to traditional social structures. This is the most complete revolution. I know that some may object that the Islamic powers do use the most modern techniques in warfare and petroleum exploitation, and, I would add, transport. . . . All this is accurate, but in Islam, technique does not dominate society. Society is always and before all else *religious*. Religion has power over everything. The question that remains before us is to see which will win out: the "Islamists," or the moderating trends and secularizing movements of the state. If the former, we will have the first worldwide victory of a revolution, but at the cost of the world's total enslavement. For Islam is equivalent to what communism was, in its will for absolute domination of the entire world.

2. A title for Mao Zedong.

3. Roger Garaudy (1913–2012), a French communist writer who converted from Christianity to Islam.

NOTE 2

Footnote 22 on page 28 indicates the point where this note belongs.

I cannot analyze all of the political orientations that churches have taken since this book was written. In any case, it can be said that contrary to the time around 1945, politics has become the principal preoccupation of a great number of churches and international Christian organizations (the World Council of Churches, for example). These churches' tendencies are simple: because one must be on the side of the poor and oppressed, the churches have become involved in all of the so-called "liberation" struggles, whether in Vietnam or Africa. They have sometimes supported communist movements, *automatically* and thoughtlessly taken the side of peoples of color, and often provided aid to "revolutionary" movements.

But, as these stances were the result of people who understood nothing about politics, who were uninformed about the tactical and strategic principles of communism and unaware that those around Lenin, for example, were already studying how to use colonized peoples to destroy capitalist power by creating social unrest, they found themselves in completely erroneous and irresponsible positions.[4] I say irresponsible, because once "revolutionary war" was won and the colonizers were driven out, then *in every country* (except where decolonization was not the result of war but of peaceful negotiation without "revolution," as in Senegal), dictatorships were established, either as pure and simple dictatorships (in Central African Republic, Libya, Uganda, etc.), generally bloody, or communist regimes were set up that were much more oppressive than the colonial regime had ever been (in Vietnam, Cambodia, Laos, Ethiopia, Angola, Congo, etc.).

When I say that these churches and the World Council of Churches are irresponsible, it is because once one of these dictatorships is set up, when there are massacres, and so on . . . these churches and Council do not denounce them—do not admit their mistakes—do not repent. Instead, they condemn the European presence somewhere new (for example, in Israel or South Africa), being sure that they are on the right side, that of the poor (which is false), and without caring about the consequences, despite all the past experiences. The example of Rhodesia is particularly clear, but no one among the leaders of these churches wants to recognize it in their struggle

---

4. Vladimir Lenin (1870–1924), communist leader of Russia or the Soviet Union from 1917 until his death.

against South Africa.[5] They understand nothing, learn nothing, and believe they are just, while they create everywhere the greatest injustices.

This is why I am completely hostile to most liberation theologies (for there isn't *one!*). Of course it is obvious that a revolution must occur in Latin America, several revolutions: at the political level, against the dictators (on the right or the left), at the economic level (by transforming the structures and the relationship with the multinational companies), at the social level (by eliminating the unacceptable exploitation whose victims are mostly the peasants), and at the ecological level (in order to struggle against the devastation of the earth's riches and forest . . .). But this cannot be done through violence or communist action. (Of course, I am also hostile to the violent struggle of the right, for example, the Contras.[6]) Here the churches would have a great revolutionary role to play, but they have not realized it, because they do not have enough political maturity.

5. The independence of Rhodesia (today Zimbabwe) did not result in the liberation of the poor but in the entrenchment of white minority rule.

6. A right-wing guerilla group active in the 1980s and 1990s that opposed the left-wing Sandinista government of Nicaragua.

Introduction to Jacques Ellul's
Life and Thought

Where does one begin with an author of more than fifty books? To make the challenge even greater, this author famously said, "I haven't written fifty books; I wrote one book with fifty chapters."[1] In this case, that of Jacques Ellul, it can safely be said that you hold in your hands the answer: *Presence in the Modern World*. One of the first books he wrote, *Presence* sketches out the core ideas of both his sociology and his theology.

Jacques Ellul was born (1912), lived, and died (1994) in Bordeaux in southwestern France. Thus, in a nation with a dominating powerful center, namely Paris, Ellul was on the geographic margins. In the shadow of a dominating Roman Catholic tradition, he was a Reformed Protestant. In an increasingly secularized culture, he was a believer and church leader. In an era of extreme specialization, he was an intellectual swashbuckler exploring and influencing many different academic fields. Little wonder then that his life and work might best be described as those of a prophet from outside, or at least from the margins, of society, culture, academy, and church.

Ellul was an only child, raised in a family that had been hard hit economically. His father, Joseph Ellul, was a Voltairean agnostic and his mother, Marthe, a Protestant believer who, out of respect for her husband, did not attend church. Ellul spent his youth hanging out among the dockworkers at the Bordeaux port on the Garonne River. He began earning his own living at age fifteen or sixteen and continued to be self-supporting through his university years by tutoring students in Latin, Greek, German, and French. He graduated from the Lycée Michel de Montaigne in 1928

---

1. When he said this it was more like thirty-five books, not yet fifty or sixty. (DG)

and then studied at the University of Bordeaux, eventually earning the doctor of laws degree in 1936 with a dissertation on the law of ancient Rome.

During his university days, beginning around 1931, Ellul read Karl Marx's *Das Kapital* and decided that it explained the economic crises (a worldwide depression) of the time. He never became a member of the Communist Party because it seemed to him far from what Marx had written, but throughout his career Ellul taught courses on Marx and his successors. Around the same time that he discovered Marx, he began to investigate Christianity and was, as a result of reading the Bible, converted with "a certain brutality." The story of his actual conversion experience is still somewhat of an intriguing mystery, but it is safe to say that the role of individual Bible study in the process pointed him toward his intense and persistent lifelong study and writing on the Hebrew and Christian Scriptures and his inclination toward the Word-centered Reformed tradition of Karl Barth. The influence of Marx continued, although it was more the sociological *method* of Marx (and for that matter, the great European sociologists such as Max Weber and Emile Durkheim) that shaped him (over against the statistical sociology characteristic of the American schools). For Ellul, then, a major question was whether one can be both a Christian and a Marxist; by the late 1930s he says he "chose decisively for faith in Christ."

In 1937, Ellul married Yvette Lensvelt, and this lifelong love continued to her death in 1991. Together they had four children, one of whom died in childhood. The three surviving children have worked to preserve and disseminate their late father's writings.

Following his doctorate, Ellul participated briefly in the Spanish Civil War, taught at Montpellier for a year, then transferred to the University of Strasbourg in 1938. In 1940 following the German occupation of France, he was fired for opposing the collaborating Vichy government. From 1940 to 1944, the Elluls lived on a farm outside of Bordeaux, working with the French Resistance (often by forging papers to protect Jews). During these years, Ellul also studied theology with the Strasbourg faculty (exiled during the war to Clermont-Ferrand in the south of France). He completed all the work for a theology degree except the final thesis by the time of the Liberation in 1944. After the Liberation, Ellul briefly worked with the Bordeaux city mayor's office but quickly despaired of its bureaucracy and corruption.

In 1944, Ellul was appointed Professor of the History and Sociology of Institutions in the faculty of law and economic sciences at the University of Bordeaux, a post he continued to hold until his retirement in 1980.

From 1947 on, he also held a chair in the Institute of Political Studies at the university. His five-volume *Histoire des institutions* (political, legal, and economic institutions from ancient Greece and Rome to World War I) was a standard university text, going through many editions, for decades.

Outside of the university classroom, Ellul was known as an advocate for students (notably during the 1968 demonstrations). He led a film discussion group in Bordeaux from 1945 to 1955. In 1958 he co-founded with Yves Charrier one of the first French clubs for the prevention of juvenile delinquency, often spending time with the street gangs and helping in their legal cases. Beginning in 1968 he was involved in the Committee for the Defense of the Aquitaine Coast on the Atlantic Ocean—trying to prevent its total takeover by construction and "development" proponents. Ellul was a frequent columnist and essayist for the regional newspapers *Sud-Ouest* and *Ouest-France* and for the national paper *Le Monde*.

Ellul's Christian faith also led him into some early participation in the World Council of Churches Committee on Work—but he left this in the early 1950s after a few years of frustration that its social research was inadequate and the theology was lacking a robust biblical orientation. He also got involved in the national leadership of the Reformed Church of France from roughly 1951 to 1970. Among his projects was a study that developed an innovative proposal for theological and seminary education—but this was never adopted because of administrative and faculty unwillingness to change. More satisfying was his role as editor of the Protestant theological journal *Foi et Vie* from 1969 to 1986.

On the local level, a small Reformed house church began in his living room and eventually moved into a chapel built by the members on property next to the Ellul home (it closed after his death in 1994). Ellul often preached sermons and led worship at his home church and spoke at other parishes and university student Christian groups. Many of his weeknight lectures on various parts of the Bible were recorded and are now being transcribed and published. Ellul also organized various associations of Protestant professionals (in banking, medicine, law, etc.), beginning in the 1950s, where lay Christians could reflect on the meaning of their biblical faith for their work.

Ellul's literary output was extraordinary, first for its volume: now nearing sixty books and over one thousand published articles. He wrote in longhand and hired a typist for all of his writings. Some inevitable errors of reference and repetition of content appear in his writings, but this is hardly a surprise given the volume and the fact that as a university professor his work was accepted and published without much editorial attention or push-back. Second, Ellul's corpus is distinctive for the range of its subject matter: history, sociology, politics, art, communications, religion, and ethics. His perspectives were and are often challenging to the conventional wisdom. But all who interacted with him, whether in print or in person, will attest that when one challenged or questioned him on some topic, he could always move to deeper levels of research and evidence for a given argument he had made.

Three keys to the appreciation and understanding of Ellul are his focus on main currents, his prophetic vocation and style, and his dialectical thinking. Ellul used the ocean as a metaphor for our potential foci of attention. On the surface of the ocean are the waves and storms; at the opposite level are the dark, still depths; and in between are the main currents (such as the Arctic Current). For anyone who is caught in a storm, the surface events are of critical importance, of course. And the sepulchral depths are also important in their own way. But it is the great main currents that give rise to the surface action. Ellul was critical of scholarship that focused too much on current events, statistics, and individual crises. And he was not much interested in the deep explorations of metaphysics. He was interested in the main currents that drive history and society. These include the growth and dominance of technique or technology, the growth of the bureaucratic state, the reduction of communication to propaganda (or trivia), and so on. In his theological and biblical studies one also notes his interest in broader themes such as the city, money, and violence, which cut across the canon. So it is important not to get stuck on any one specific point asserted by Ellul and then miss out on consideration of these broader flows, whether sociological or theological.

Second, Ellul is best understood as a kind of prophet rather than a systematic teacher. He is not a prophet to the masses but a prophet to intellectuals, to people who think, who care, who read and listen and lead. He often said that he did not seek or want followers; he wanted only to provide his readers with resources to help them think out for themselves the meaning of their lives. Like most prophets, Ellul's writings are sometimes harsh and brash and upsetting. Most of us who have studied Ellul (or even studied with Ellul) can point to various places where we disagree (or even argued with Ellul himself) on various issues. But all of us would say he was one of the greatest people we have ever studied (with), and that our engagement with him and his works always made us think more deeply and better. In person, he was a gentle man with a kind smile and a twinkle in his eye.

Third, Ellul often explained that his thinking and work were inextricably dialectical. He argued that history and learning and theology and life itself are all best understood in a dialectical fashion. What this means is that truth and reality are not linear and axiomatic-deductive. We have to see the thesis and antithesis, the point and counter point, the positive and negative. We cannot create some intellectual synthesis but must resolve the dialectic in our *life*. We can *live* with the dialectic even though we cannot intellectually resolve it in a simple way. Remember how we learned that light can be described through wave theory or particle theory—but not through some hybrid "wavicle" model. And in theology, God is one and God is three, but not resolvable as a God in "thirds." Jesus is fully human and fully divine, not half and half. Humans are simultaneously sinful and redeemed, old life and new life. So, too, the state is simultaneously a demonic threat and an expression of human community; the city is Babylon and Jerusalem.

In this way, Ellul is closer to Kierkegaard than to Marx or Hegel when it comes to dialectic.[2] Marx argued for a dialectical materialism that would resolve itself in the historical emergence of a classless society. Hegel saw a dialectical progress in the mind and spirit of the age. Kierkegaard, however, proposed a dialectical resolution in our *existence* moment by moment (hence, "existentialism"). It is no surprise that Kierkegaard was Ellul's favorite thinker. So if you like simple, unconflicting elaborations of a position or argument, you won't find them in Ellul. He will boldly argue for a contrary position that he feels needs to be articulated in our era. In some cases he will hold up the other pole of the dialectic. For example, Christians are "in the world" but "not of the world." In other cases he will argue mostly or only for one pole (the modern city is Babylon under the power of Satan with a will to suicide) and not provide the other, because it already has overwhelming support in the culture (e.g., Urbanization is good! Technology is the answer!).

Dialectic was not only Ellul's intellectual orientation, it was his personal choice. Throughout his life, his closest friend and intellectual partner was Bernard Charbonneau, never a believer, living in the foothills of

2. Soren Kierkegaard (1813–55) and Georg Wilhelm Friedrich Hegel (1770–1831), philosophers.

the Pyrenees and not metropolitan Bordeaux, an independent intellectual rather than university professor. Clearly they had much in common, but the dialectical interplay of these two great minds has a great deal to do with the fruitfulness of Ellul's thought (and Charbonneau's as well). It is no accident that the community of minds that is the International Jacques Ellul Society is, by all accounts, the most diverse and lively—and rewarding—community in which any of its members participate. We welcome you to join the conversation.

David W. Gill
2016
Berkeley, California

Bibliography of Books
by Jacques Ellul

ELLUL'S BOOKS IN ENGLISH TRANSLATION

Anarchy and Christianity. Translated by Geoffrey W. Bromiley. Grand Rapids: Eerdmans, 1991; Eugene, OR: Wipf and Stock, 2011. Originally published as *Anarchie et christianisme.* Lyon: Atelier de Création Libertaire, 1988; Paris: Table Ronde, 1998, 2001.

Apocalypse: The Book of Revelation. Translated by George W. Schreiner. New York: Seabury, 1977. Originally published as *L'Apocalypse: Architecture en mouvement.* Paris: Desclée, 1975; Geneva: Labor et Fides, 2008; Paris: Cerf, 2008.

Autopsy of Revolution. Translated by Patricia Wolf. New York: Knopf, 1971; Eugene, OR: Wipf and Stock, 2012. Originally published as *Autopsie de la révolution.* Paris: Calmann-Lévy, 1969; Paris: Table Ronde, 2008.

The Betrayal of the West. Translated by Matthew J. O'Connell. New York: Seabury, 1978. Originally published as *Trahison de l'Occident.* Paris: Calmann-Lévy, 1975; Paris: Princi Negue, 2003.

A Critique of the New Commonplaces. Translated by Helen Weaver. New York: Knopf, 1968; Eugene, OR: Wipf and Stock, 2012. Originally published as *Exégèse des nouveaux lieux communs.* Paris: Calmann-Lévy, 1966; Paris: Table Ronde, 1994, 2004.

The Empire of Non-Sense: Art in the Technological Society. Translated by Michael Johnson and David Lovekin. Winterbourne, UK: Papadakis, 2014. Originally published as *L'Empire du non-sens: L'Art et la société technicienne.* Paris: Presses Universitaires de France, 1980.

The Ethics of Freedom. Translated by Geoffrey W. Bromiley. Grand Rapids: Eerdmans, 1976; London: Mowbrays, 1976. (A translation of volume 1 and of an early draft of part of volume 3.) Originally published as *Éthique de la liberté.* V. 1, Paris: Librairie Protestante, 1973; Geneva: Labor et Fides, 1973. V. 2, 1974. V. 3 (*Les Combats de la liberté*), Geneva: Labor et Fides, 1984; Paris: Centurion, 1984.

False Presence of the Kingdom. Translated by C. Edward Hopkin. New York: Seabury, 1972. Originally published as *Fausse présence au monde moderne.* Paris: Les Bergers et Les Mages, 1963; Paris: Librairie Protestante, 1963.

Hope in Time of Abandonment. Translated by C. Edward Hopkin. New York: Seabury, 1973; Eugene, OR: Wipf and Stock, 2012. Originally published as *L'Espérance oubliée.* Paris: Gallimard, 1972; Paris: Table Ronde, 2004.

The Humiliation of the Word. Translated by Joyce Main Hanks. Grand Rapids: Eerdmans, 1985. Originally published as *La Parole humiliée.* Paris: Seuil, 1981; Paris: Table Ronde, 2014.

If You Are the Son of God: The Suffering and Temptations of Jesus. Translated by Anne-Marie Andreasson-Hogg. Eugene, OR: Wipf and Stock, 2014. Originally published as *Si tu es le Fils de Dieu: Souffrances et tentations de Jésus.* Paris: Centurion, 1991.

Islam and Judeo-Christianity: A Critique of Their Commonality. Translated by D. Bruce MacKay. Eugene, OR: Wipf and Stock, 2015. (Includes a chapter on Islam from *The Subversion of Christianity.*) Originally published as *Islam et judéo-christianisme: texte inédit.* Edited by Alain Besançon. Paris: Presses Universitaires de France, 2004, 2006.

Jesus and Marx: From Gospel to Ideology. Translated by Joyce Main Hanks. Grand Rapids: Eerdmans, 1988; Eugene, OR: Wipf and Stock, 2012. Originally published as *L'Idéologie marxiste chrétienne: Que fait-on de l'Évangile?* Paris: Centurion, 1979; Paris: Table Ronde, 2006.

The Judgment of Jonah. Translated by Geoffrey W. Bromiley. Grand Rapids: Eerdmans, 1971; Eugene, OR: Wipf and Stock, 2011. Originally published as *Le Livre de Jonas.* Paris: Cahiers Bibliques de Foi et Vie, 1952.

Living Faith: Belief and Doubt in a Perilous World. Translated by Peter Heinegg. San Francisco: Harper and Row, 1983; Eugene, OR: Wipf and Stock, 2012. Originally published as *La Foi au prix du doute: "Encore quarante jours . . ."* Paris: Hachette, 1980; Paris: Table Ronde, 2015.

The Meaning of the City. Translated by Dennis Pardee. Grand Rapids: Eerdmans, 1970; Carlisle, UK: Paternoster, 1997; Eugene, OR: Wipf and Stock, 2011. Originally published as *Sans feu ni lieu: Signification biblique de la Grande Ville.* Paris: Gallimard, 1975; Paris: Table Ronde.

Money and Power. Translated by LaVonne Neff. Downers Grove, IL: IVP, 1984; Basingstoke, UK: Marshall Pickering, 1986; Eugene, OR: Wipf and Stock, 2009. Originally published as *L'Homme et l'argent (Nova et vetera).* Neuchâtel: Delachaux & Niestlé, 1954; Lausanne: Presses Bibliques Universitaires, 1979.

The New Demons. Translated by C. Edward Hopkin. New York: Seabury, 1975; London: Mowbrays, 1975. Originally published as *Les Nouveaux possédés.* Paris: Fayard, 1973; Paris: Mille et une nuits, 2003.

On Being Rich and Poor: Christianity in a Time of Economic Globalization. Compiled, edited, and translated by Willem H. Vanderburg. Toronto: University of Toronto Press, 2014. (Based on recordings of Ellul's Bible studies of Amos and James and interviews with the translator/editor.)

On Freedom, Love, and Power. Compiled, edited, and translated by Willem H. Vanderburg. Toronto: University of Toronto Press, 2010. (Based on recordings of Ellul's Bible studies of passages in Genesis, Job, Matthew, and John and interviews with the translator/editor.)

The Political Illusion. Translated by Konrad Kellen. New York: Knopf, 1967; New York: Random, 1972; Eugene, OR: Wipf and Stock, 2015. Originally published as *L'Illusion politique.* Paris: Robert Laffont, 1965; Paris: Livre de poche, 1977; Rev. ed., Paris: Librairie Générale Française, 1977; Paris: Table Ronde, 2004, 2012.

The Politics of God and the Politics of Man. Translated by Geoffrey W. Bromiley. Grand Rapids: Eerdmans, 1972; Eugene, OR: Wipf and Stock, 2012. Originally published as *Politique de Dieu, politiques de l'homme.* Paris: Éditions Universitaires, 1966.

Prayer and Modern Man. Translated by C. Edward Hopkin. New York: Seabury, 1970, 1973; Eugene, OR: Wipf and Stock, 2012. Originally published as *L'Impossible prière.* Paris: Centurion, 1971, 1977.

The Presence of the Kingdom. Translated by Olive Wyon. Philadelphia: Westminster, 1951; London: SCM, 1951; New York: Seabury, 1967; Colorado Springs: Helmers & Howard, 1989. Originally published as *Présence au monde moderne: Problèmes de la civilisation post-chrétienne.* Geneva: Roulet, 1948; Lausanne: Presses Bibliques Universitaires, 1988; Lausanne: Ouverture, 1988.

Propaganda: The Formation of Men's Attitudes. Translated by Konrad Kellen and Jean Lerner. New York: Knopf, 1965; New York: Random, 1973. Originally published as *Propagandes.* Paris: Armand Colin, 1962; Paris: Économica, 1990, 2008.

Reason for Being: A Meditation on Ecclesiastes. Translated by Joyce Main Hanks. Grand Rapids: Eerdmans, 1990. Originally published as *La Raison d'être: Méditation sur l'Ecclésiaste.* Paris: Seuil, 1987, 1995; Paris: Points, 2007.

Sources and Trajectories: Eight Early Articles by Jacques Ellul that Set the Stage. Translated by Marva J. Dawn. Grand Rapids: Eerdmans, 1997.

The Subversion of Christianity. Translated by Geoffrey W. Bromiley. Grand Rapids: Eerdmans, 1986; Eugene, OR: Wipf and Stock, 2011. Originally published as *La Subversion du christianisme.* Paris: Seuil, 1984, 1994; Paris: Table Ronde, 2001, 2012.

The Technological Bluff. Translated by Geoffrey W. Bromiley. Grand Rapids: Eerdmans, 1990. Originally published as *Le Bluff technologique.* Paris: Hachette, 1988, 1990, 2004; Paris: Pluriel, 2012.

The Technological Society. Translated by John Wilkinson. New York: Knopf, 1964; London: Jonathan Cape, 1965; Rev. ed., New York: Knopf, 1967. Originally published as *La Technique ou l'enjeu du siècle.* Paris: Armand Colin, 1954; Paris: Économica, 1990, 2008.

The Technological System. Translated by Joachim Neugroschel. New York: Continuum, 1980. Originally published as *Le Système technicien.* Paris: Calmann-Lévy, 1977; Paris: Cherche-midi, 2004, 2012.

The Theological Foundation of Law. Translated by Marguerite Wieser. Garden City, NY: Doubleday, 1960; London: SCM, 1961; New York: Seabury, 1969. Originally published as *Le Fondement théologique du droit.* Neuchâtel: Delachaux & Niestlé, 1946; Paris: Dalloz, 2008.

To Will and To Do: An Ethical Research for Christians. Translated by C. Edward Hopkin. Philadelphia: Pilgrim, 1969. Originally published as *Le Vouloir et le faire: Recherches éthiques pour les chrétiens.* Geneva: Labor et Fides, 1964; Paris: Librairie Protestante, 1964, 2013.

An Unjust God? A Christian Theology of Israel in Light of Romans 9–11. Translated by Anne-Marie Andreasson-Hogg. Eugene, OR: Wipf and Stock, 2012. Originally published as *Ce Dieu injuste—? Théologie chrétienne pour le peuple d'Israël.* Paris: Arléa, 1991, 1999.

Violence: Reflections from a Christian Perspective. Translated by Cecelia Gaul Kings. New York: Seabury, 1969; London: SCM, 1970; London: Mowbrays, 1978; Eugene, OR: Wipf and Stock, 2012. Originally published as *Contre les violents.* Paris: Centurion, 1972.

What I Believe. Translated by Geoffrey W. Bromiley. Grand Rapids: Eerdmans, 1989. Originally published as *Ce que je crois.* Paris: Grasset & Fasquelle, 1987, 1989.

ELLUL'S BOOKS IN FRENCH (NO ENGLISH TRANSLATION)

Changer de révolution: L'Inéluctable prolétariat. [Change of Revolution: The Ineluctable Proletariat.] Paris: Seuil, 1982; Paris: Table Ronde, 2015.

Conférence sur l'Apocalypse de Jean. [Lectures on the Revelation of John.] Nantes: Association pour la Recherche, l'Enseignement, la Formation, la Pratique de la Psychanalyse, 1985. (Transcript of lectures given November 3–4, 1984.)

De la révolution aux révoltes. [From Revolution to Revolts.] Paris: Calmann-Lévy, 1972; Paris: Table Ronde, 2011.

Le Défi et le nouveau: Œuvres théologiques, 1948–1991. [The Challenge and the New: Theological Works, 1948–1991.] Paris: Table Ronde, 2007. (A reprint of eight of Ellul's theological books: *Présence au monde moderne, Le Livre de Jonas, L'Homme et l'argent, Politique de Dieu, politiques de l'homme, Contre les violents, L'Impossible prière, Un Chrétien pour Israël,* and *Si tu es le Fils de Dieu.*)

Déviances et déviants dans notre société intolérante. [Deviancy and Deviants in Our Intolerant Society.] Toulouse: Érés, 1992, 2013.

Essai sur le recrutement de l'armée française au XVIe et XVIIe siècles. [Essay on the Recruitment of the French Army in the Sixteenth and Seventeenth Centuries.] Mémoires de l'académie des sciences morales, 1941.

Étude sur l'évolution et la nature juridique du Mancipium. [Study on the Juridical Development and Nature of the Mancipium.] Bordeaux: Delmas, 1936. (Ellul's doctoral thesis.)

La Genèse aujourd'hui. [The Book of Genesis for Today.] With François Tosquelles. Nantes: Association pour la Recherche, l'Enseignement, la Formation, la Pratique de la Psychanalyse, 1987. (Transcript of lectures on Genesis 1 and 2, given November 30–December 1, 1985.)

Histoire de la propagande. [A History of Propaganda.] Paris: Presses Universitaires de France, 1967, 1976.

Histoire des institutions. [A History of Institutions.] Paris: Presses Universitaires de France. Vol. 1–2, *L'Antiquité* [Antiquity], 1955, 1972, 1999. Vol. 3, *Le Moyen Age* [The Middle Ages], 1956, 1975, 1980, 1999, 2006. Vol. 4, *Les XVIe–XVIIIe siècles* [The Sixteenth through Eighteenth Centuries], 1956, 1976, 1999. Vol. 5, *Le XIXe siècle 1789–1914* [The Nineteenth Century, 1789–1914], 1956, 1979, 1999.

Introduction à l'histoire de la discipline des Églises réformées de France. [Introduction to the History of the Discipline of the Reformed Churches of France.] 1943.

Israël: Chance de civilisation: articles de journaux et de revues, 1967–1992. [Israel: A Chance for Civilization: Newspaper and Journal Articles, 1967–1992.] Paris: Éditions Première Partie, 2008.

Jeunesse délinquante: Une expérience en province. [Delinquent Youth: A Rural Experience]. With Yves Charrier. Paris: Mercure de France, 1971; 2nd ed., *Jeunesse délinquante: Des blousons noirs aux hippies.* [Delinquent Youth: From Toughs to Hippies.] Nantes:

Association pour la Recherche, l'Enseignement, la Formation, la Pratique de la Psychanalyse, 1985.

Métamorphose du bourgeois. [Metamorphosis of the Bourgeoisie.] Paris: Calmann-Lévy, 1967; Paris: Table Ronde, 1998, 2012.

Oratorio: Les quatre cavaliers de l'Apocalypse. [Oratorio: The Four Horsemen of the Apocalypse.] Bordeaux: Opales, 1997. (Poems.)

La pensée marxiste: Cours professé à l'Institut d'études politiques de Bordeaux de 1947 à 1979. [Marxist Thought: A Course Taught at the Institute for Political Studies of Bordeaux from 1947 to 1979.] Edited by Michel Hourcade, Jean-Pierre Jézéquel, and Gérard Paul. Paris: Table Ronde, 2003, 2011. (Course notes from three of Ellul's students.)

Penser globalement, agir localement: chroniques journalistiques. [Think Globally, Act Locally: Newspaper Columns.] Cressé: Éditions des Regionalismes, 2007, 2009. (Articles and columns published between 1953 and 1991 in the regional newspapers *Sud-ouest* and *Ouest-France.*)

Pour qui, pour quoi travaillons-nous? [Who and What Are We Working For?] Compiled and edited by Michel Hourcade, Jean-Pierre Jézéquel, and Gérard Paul. Paris: Table Ronde, 2013.

Silences: Poèmes. [Silences: Poems.] Bordeaux: Opales, 1995.

Les successeurs de Marx: Cours professé à l'Institut d'études politiques de Bordeaux. [Marx's Successors: A Course Taught at the Institute for Political Studies of Bordeaux.] Edited by Michel Hourcade, Jean-Pierre Jézéquel, and Gérard Paul. Paris: Table Ronde, 2007. (Course notes from three of Ellul's students.)

Théologie et technique: Pour une éthique de la non-puissance. [Theology and Technique: For an Ethic of Non-Power.] Edited by Yves Ellul and Frédéric Rognon. Geneva: Labor et Fides, 2014.

Un chrétien pour Israël. [A Christian for Israel.] Monaco: Éditions du Rocher, 1986.

INTERVIEWS PUBLISHED IN BOOK FORM

L'homme à lui-même: Correspondance. [The Man to Himself: Letters.] With Didier Nordon. Paris: Félin, 1992.

In Season, Out of Season: An Introduction to the Thought of Jacques Ellul: Interviews by Madeleine Garrigou-Lagrange. Translated by Lani K. Niles. San Francisco: Harper and Row, 1982. Originally published as *À temps et à contretemps: Entretiens avec Madeleine Garrigou-Lagrange.* Paris: Centurion, 1981.

Jacques Ellul on Politics, Technology, and Christianity. Eugene, OR: Wipf and Stock, 2005. Previously published as *Jacques Ellul on Religion, Technology, and Politics: Conversations with Patrick Troude-Chastenet.* Translated by Joan Mendès France. Atlanta: Scholars, 1998. Originally published as *Entretiens avec Jacques Ellul.* With Patrick Chastenet. Paris: Table Ronde, 1994. Rev. ed., *À Contre-courant: Entretiens,* 2014.

Perspectives on Our Age: Jacques Ellul Speaks on His Life and Work. Edited by William H. Vanderburg. Translated by Joachim Neugroschel. Toronto: CBC, 1981; New York: Seabury, 1981; Concord, ON: Anansi, 1997, 2004.

SELECTED RESOURCES FOR THE STUDY OF JACQUES ELLUL

The Ellul Forum for the Critique of Technological Civilization, www.ellul.org. (Published twice yearly since 1988.)

Goddard, Andrew. *Living the Word, Resisting the World: The Life and Thought of Jacques Ellul*. Paternoster Theological Monographs. Carlisle UK: Paternoster, 2002.

Hanks, Joyce Main. *The Reception of Jacques Ellul's Critique of Technology: An Annotated Bibliography of Writings on His Life and Thought*. Lewiston, NY: Mellen, 2007.

————. *Jacques Ellul: An Annotated Bibliography of Primary Works*, Research in Philosophy and Technology, supp. 5. Stamford, CT: JAI, 2000.

————. *Jacques Ellul: A Comprehensive Bibliography. Update, 1985–1993*. Research in Philosophy and Technology, vol. 15. Stamford, CT: JAI, 1995.

————. *Jacques Ellul: A Comprehensive Bibliography. Update, 1982–1985*. Research in Philosophy and Technology, vol. 11. Stamford, CT: JAI, 1991.

————. *Jacques Ellul: A Comprehensive Bibliography*. Research in Philosophy and Technology, supp. 1. Stamford, CT: JAI, 1984.

Jacques Ellul: L'Homme entier. [Jacques Ellul: The Complete Man.] Film produced by Serge Steyer. Paris: Promenade en mer, 1995.

Porquet, Jean-Luc. *L'Homme qui avait presque tout prévu*. [The Man Who Foretold Almost Everything.] Paris: Cherche-Midi, 2003.

Rognon, Frédéric. *Générations Ellul: Soixante héritiers de la pensée de Jacques Ellul*. [Ellul Generations: Sixty Heirs of Jacques Ellul's Thought.] Geneva: Labor et Fides, 2012.

The Treachery of Technology. [Het verraad van de techniek.] Film produced by Jan van Boeckel. Amsterdam: Rerun Productions, 1992.

Troude-Chastenet, Patrick. *Lire Ellul: Introduction à l'œuvre socio-politique de Jacques Ellul*. [Reading Ellul: Introduction to the Socio-Political Work of Jacques Ellul.] Talence: Presses Universitaires de Bordeaux, 1992.

JACQUES ELLUL SOCIETY INFORMATION

The International Jacques Ellul Society (English) and Association Internationale Jacques Ellul (French) are sister organizations that were founded in the year 2000. Their websites at www.ellul.org and www.jacques-ellul.org provide extensive information about Ellul's life and writings, conferences, resources, and more.

Topical Index

War, 5, 13, 17, 19, 23, 43–45, 67, 104,
105
nuclear, 66
and the event, 76
Second World War, xv–xx, 12
Weber, Max, xix

World, oriented to action, 59
its preservation, 12–15, 26, 29, 36
its will to death, 14–16, 18, 23–28,
37, 47
World Council of Churches, 105

Scripture Index

17018370R00089

Printed in Poland
by Amazon Fulfillment
Poland Sp. z o.o., Wrocław